Adams Media
An Imprint of Simon & Schuster, Inc.
100 Technology Center Drive
Stoughton, Massachusetts 02072

First Adams Media hardcover edition November 2023

ADAMS MEDIA and colophon are registered trademarks of Simon & Schuster, Inc.

TASTY HOME is a trademark of BuzzFeed Media Enterprises, Inc., and used under license. All rights reserved.

For information about special discounts for bulk purchases, please contact Simon & Schuster Special Sales at 1-866-506-1949 or business@simonandschuster.com.

The Simon & Schuster Speakers Bureau can bring authors to your live event. For more information or to book an event, contact the Simon & Schuster Speakers Bureau at 1-866-248-3049 or visit our website at www.simonspeakers.com.

Interior design by Sylvia McArdle
Photographs © Getty Images; 123RF; BuzzFeed Media Enterprises, Inc.
Illustrations © BuzzFeed Media Enterprises, Inc.

Manufactured in China

10 9 8 7 6 5 4 3 2 1

Library of Congress Cataloging-in-Publication Data
Title: Tasty™ Home: life skills: / Tasty™ Home.
Other titles: Tasty™ Home (Website)
Description: Stoughton, Massachusetts: Adams Media, [2023] | Includes index.
Identifiers: LCCN 2023006315 | ISBN 9781507216026 (hc) | ISBN 9781507216033 (ebook)
Subjects: LCSH: Life skills. | House cleaning. | Storage in the home. | Orderliness.
Classification: LCC HQ2037 .N54 2023 | DDC 646.7--dc23/eng/20230221
LC record available at https://lccn.loc.gov/2023006315

ISBN 978-1-5072-1602-6
ISBN 978-1-5072-1603-3 (ebook)

Contents

CHAPTER 1

Cleaning &
Organizing

GET THROUGH YOUR CHORES ASAP

Whether you live in a house, an apartment, a shared room, or a New York City closet that rents for the GDP of a small nation, you need to keep your space **clean** and **organized**. Once you get good at cleaning and organizing, you might even start to enjoy it—or at least the feeling of having done it. This chapter is full of cleaning and organizing basics—as well as some little tips, hacks, and DIY ideas—to help you get there.

Cleaning vs. Disinfecting vs. Sanitizing

These words are often used interchangeably, but they're not synonyms. It's important to know the difference so you can keep your surfaces are clean *and* safe. Per the Centers for Disease Control and Prevention:

- **Cleaning** means using soap and water on a surface. Cleaning won't kill all germs, but it does reduce their number.
- **Disinfecting** means using chemicals to kill germs on a surface. Disinfectants don't always clean surfaces, so if you're trying to keep your household healthy, you need to clean *and* disinfect.
- **Sanitizing** means reducing germs to a level that's been deemed safe by public health requirements, and may be done by cleaning, disinfecting, or both.

   Now you can tell your friends about that distinction and get a reputation for being real fun at parties.

Love Your Pets— Not Their Messes

Pets are lucky they're so adorable because they can be truly disgusting. Here are some tips to clean up their mess:

- Line cat litter boxes with plastic bags before pouring in litter for easier cleaning.
- To remove lingering smells from couches and chairs, sprinkle with baking soda and let sit for 30 minutes. Then vacuum up the scent-absorbing powder.
- Run your rubber-glove-clad hands or a squeegee over upholstered furniture and curtains to remove pet hair. Or use anything sticky, like duct tape or a lint roller.
- Some pet toys can go in the dishwasher with a tablespoon of white vinegar instead of detergent. Put soft toys in the washing machine with a sprinkle of baking soda and a tablespoon of white vinegar instead of detergent.

Opt for Natural DIY Cleaners

Many natural cleaning all-stars are primarily known as food items: baking soda, white vinegar, and lemon juice. When you're shopping for these items as cleansers, you do not need the pricey stuff. Brand-name baking soda, fancy bottles of vinegar, and organic lemons won't clean any better, so save your money. To streamline your cleaning process, keep natural cleansers and DIY detergents in clearly labeled containers, e.g., white vinegar in a handy spray bottle.

Clean Splatters Off Your Microwave

If your microwave looks like a kid's art class painting—and eventually, they all do—here's how to clean it quickly using what you already have in your kitchen. Cut two lemons into slices and place them in a microwave-safe bowl filled halfway with water. Put the bowl in the microwave and heat until the water boils. Slip on oven mitts and remove the bowl (it will be hot!), then use a sponge to wipe off the grime, which should now be softened for easy cleaning.

Freshen Up Your Grout

Grout: You really only notice it when it's dirty (which seems to be often). Clean it up with a mix of equal parts water and white vinegar. Just spray it on, let it sit for 10 minutes, then scrub with a brush. For tougher mildew or grime, apply a baking soda and water paste first, and then spray on the water and vinegar mixture. The last-ditch option if nothing else works: Buy a grout pen and color over the discoloration.

20-Minute Quick Clean Checklist

If you're new to regular cleaning and don't know where to start, here's a simple checklist you can use to clean your space *fast* when you have unexpected visitors coming:

• Put away items that are out of place (e.g., hang up your coat).

• Clean anything that's obviously messy or dirty (e.g., make the bed, wash dishes, mop up spilled coffee).

• Wipe and disinfect surfaces, especially ones used daily (e.g., countertops).

• Dust, at least in places where you see dust bunnies congregating (e.g., under furniture).

• Clean any area that gets used super frequently, especially if water is involved (e.g., sinks, toilets, and bathtubs).

• Do regular chores that aren't necessarily tied to one particular room (e.g., take out garbage).

Clean Your Phone

You probably don't even want to think about how disgusting your phone gets. To clean it, power down and remove the phone from its case. Then, mix equal parts water and 70% rubbing alcohol (or equal parts water and white vinegar) into a spray bottle. Spray onto a microfiber cloth and carefully wipe the phone. Make sure to get the screen, back, and sides, and do the case too, inside and out. For extra disinfecting, hold a UV light 2.5 inches to 3 inches above the phone for 10–15 seconds. Repeat until each part of the phone has been covered.

Clean Stained Rugs & Carpets

Many spills on carpets and rugs can be tackled with the usual suspects:

For spilled **wine**, dab with a towel, then cover the stain in white vinegar. Let sit for 15 minutes, then blot. Sprinkle with baking soda, brush with a wet toothbrush, then rinse the spot with water.

Chocolate stain? Let it harden, then scrape off excess with a knife. Mix a small amount of laundry detergent with water, pour it on the stain, and let sit for 5 minutes. Scrub with a toothbrush, blot with a towel, then rinse with water.

Soak up **coffee** stains with a towel, then pour on a mixture of laundry detergent and water. Blot until the coffee is absorbed. Finally, soak the area with white vinegar and blot. Repeat until the stain is gone, then rinse with water.

Make Stainless Steel Shine

Despite its name, stainless steel does need to be cleaned. Get your silver-toned appliances smudge-free and shiny again with a microfiber cloth and a cleanser made specifically for stainless surfaces. Or use a teaspoon of dish soap mixed with a quart of hot water. Spot-treat rust with a damp cloth dipped in baking soda. Stainless sinks and cookware, unlike appliances, can handle scrubbing with a scrub brush and mildly abrasive cleaner, like a mix of equal parts water and white vinegar, or for tougher stains, a paste of baking soda and water.

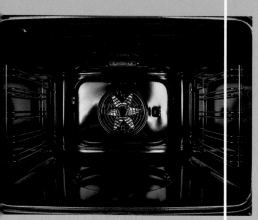

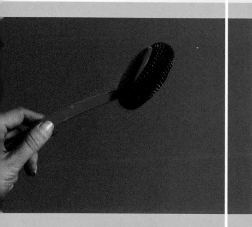

4 **Steps for Making Your Oven Sparkle the Natural Way**

Cleaning an oven feels like a major undertaking, but you can do it with some everyday pantry staples and a little elbow grease. It's worth the effort when your oven looks like new!

1. First, remove the oven racks and set aside. In a bowl, make a paste by mixing water, a teaspoon at a time, with 1 cup of baking soda. Spread the paste on the interior of the oven, avoiding heating elements, and let it sit overnight.

2. The next day, spray white vinegar over the paste, and wipe the resulting foam away with a damp sponge. Spray tougher spots with more vinegar, and scrub with a copper sponge.

3. Clean the oven racks the same way, letting the vinegar and baking soda mixture sit for a few minutes before scrubbing.

4. Finally, wipe off any remaining foam from the oven or racks with a damp cloth.

Defrost Your Freezer

Over time, freezers build up layers of ice inside them that can cause them to run inefficiently, lose space, and absorb smells. Some newer freezers defrost themselves. (How considerate!) Others just continually add ice that becomes *your* problem. (Rude!) Here's what to do if you need to defrost your freezer:

1. First, get everything out of your freezer. (Put it in the fridge or in another freezer if possible, or cook and eat it.)

2. Turn the freezer off or unplug it. (The contents of your refrigerator should stay cool for an hour or two—just try to keep the fridge door shut as you work. And if there's anything super temp-sensitive in the fridge, move that to a cooler with ice.) Remove shelves, and place towels and baking trays in the freezer to catch dripping water. Leave the freezer door open.

3. Carefully chip away any ice you can remove with a spatula. Place a bowl of hot water in the freezer to warm the space, continuing to scrape and mop up the ice as it melts.

4. Finally, clean and dry your freezer walls and shelves, put everything back, and turn the freezer back on.

Degrease Your Stovetop

Aside from wiping up frequently, sometimes, or all the time, if you cook a lot, you'll need to seriously clean your stovetop every once in a while. To deep-clean, mix a cup of baking soda with half a cup of water and a few drops of citrus essential oil. Soak paper towels in the mixture and carefully place them around the heating elements to soften grime. (If your stovetop has grates, remove them first to clean underneath.) Then add more of the mixture and scrub with the abrasive side of a sponge as needed. Wipe clean and return grates before reuse.

Clean Your Laptop

When was the last time you really looked at your keyboard and screen? It probably needs a good clean. First, turn off and unplug the computer. Then, clean the keyboard with compressed air, cleaning putty or gel, or good old cotton swabs dampened in rubbing alcohol. Clean the screen with a smooth microfiber cloth, either dry or damp.

Protect Yourself

Even the most natural, homemade cleansers can be harsh on your body. They're supposed to be tough on dirt, right? When you're cleaning, especially if you're on the sensitive side, suit up with rubber gloves, eye protection (even more so if you're applying cleanser to a surface above you), and a face mask to keep out dust. Also, open windows and doors if possible (except when dusting; you don't want that stuff to blow around).

And to avoid disaster, read the instructions and warning labels of any cleaning products you buy, and do some research before inventing your own concoctions—some common household chemicals are very dangerous when mixed.

Pace Yourself

If your image of keeping a clean home involves some perfect person or happy family thoroughly cleaning their entire house every weekend, relax! You do not have to clean every room in your house—or every corner of your tiny apartment—at the same time or with the same frequency.

High-traffic areas, and those prone to messes, should be cleaned often. But rooms that are rarely used and corners with barely any stuff in them can go much longer between cleanings. And even then, they might only need a quick wipe down most of the time.

Also, if your busy life never lets you spend hours in a row cleaning, it's totally fine to break it up and do, say, 15 minutes a day instead.

What NOT to Clean on Your Own

Yes, this chapter is all about how you can improve your cleaning skills. But there are limits! In some nasty situations, you really shouldn't attempt to clean up on your own. In these cases, it's safer to call your landlord (if you rent) or a specialized cleaning or remediation company (if you own).

Call a pro if you're dealing with spilled chemicals, mold, flooding or fire damage, sewage, animal infestation, or anything you sense might be a serious health hazard or require special equipment or training. It's better to be safe than sorry.

Use Less Soap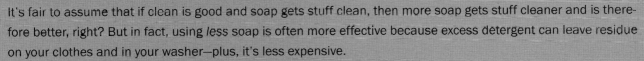

It's fair to assume that if clean is good and soap gets stuff clean, then more soap gets stuff cleaner and is therefore better, right? But in fact, using *less* soap is often more effective because excess detergent can leave residue on your clothes and in your washer—plus, it's less expensive.

For example, a small drop of detergent goes a long way when hand-washing dishes, and you don't usually need to completely fill that giant detergent bottle cap to wash your clothes. Follow the instructions on the packaging—you'll often find the recommended amount is much less than you've been using. When *should* you use a lot of soap? For thoroughly washing your hands after cleaning your home.

Avoid a Dust-Up

Whether it's the inherent silliness of feather dusters or the Halloween costume cringe of old-timey maids' uniforms, there's an old-fashioned vibe around dusting. Unfortunately, dust is still *very* much around today. If you're not dusting frequently, you should start. Fortunately, you don't need a silly duster; you can use a modern microfiber one or even a dryer sheet in a pinch. And pro tip: Always start at the top of the room and work your way down toward the floor.

5 Little Extras That Elevate Your Cleaning Routines

POV: You know how to clean; you just want to make it a little more convenient. You buy:

1. **Microfiber cloths:** These soft towels are great for surfaces like stainless steel or anything you don't want to scratch. And just throw them in the washer to clean and reuse.

2. **Magic Erasers:** These little white blocks will make all your scuffed non-glossy white surfaces, from walls to cabinets to sneakers, look brand new.

3. **Sponges on a stick:** Switch your boring old sponge for a skinny one with a long handle to tackle tall coffee mugs and reusable water bottles with ease.

4. **Straw-cleaning brushes:** Keep glass and metal straws clean with a scrubby tool made just for them.

5. **Kitchen sink suction organizers:** For a streamlined kitchen, stash your soap, sponges, and other unsightly necessities in an organizer affixed to the inside of your sink.

Deep-Clean Your Fridge

You'll have to do it eventually, so you might as well do it right. First, take everything out and toss any food that's gross or expired. Remove drawers and shelves (including the shelves in the door) and wash them in the sink with dish soap. When they're dry, clean glass shelves with spray-on glass cleaner. Dislodge stubborn crumbs from trim with the pointy end of an orange stick, that little wooden tool made for nails and cuticles.

Clean the interior of the fridge with all-purpose cleanser and a damp cloth. Replace drawers and shelves. Wipe sticky food containers (hey there, balsamic), then replace everything neatly in the fridge.

Spots You Might Be Forgetting to Clean

You cleaned the big things, like the floors and counters. But what did you miss?

- **Light switches.** Touched by so many grubby hands.
- **Doorknobs and door handles.** Ditto.
- **Yoga mats and exercise equipment.** Even if no one touches it but you, wipe that sweat off.
- **Under and around houseplants.** Like all living things, someone has to clean up after them.
- **Radiators and heating vents, registers, grills, and so on.** Because the only thing worse than dirt is *hot* dirt.
- **For pet owners and parents:** under couches and large appliances. It's not always possible to move these, but if you can, check occasionally for caches of LEGO bricks, bouncy balls, bottle caps, and toy mice.
- **Hearths.** Even if you never use your fireplace, this little patch of floor will find a way to get dirty.
- **Stairs and hallways.** Dust bunnies love these spots too.
- **Ceiling fans.** Don't wait until summer to turn them on and find out.
- **Windowsills.** Street dirt, pollen, and dust—ugh.
- **Under chairs and tables.** Especially around legs, which act as magnets for all manner of fluff.
- **Baseboards.** How does dust know to gather there? No one knows.
- **Blinds.** Yes, it's a pain to dust all those little slats. But you'll be shocked at how clean they look when you're done.
- **Books, bookshelves, and nonbook things** (including candles) displayed on bookshelves.
- **Shoes.** Any line-up of footwear—no matter how clean—will soon be surrounded by a collection of outdoor dirt. It's a life rule.

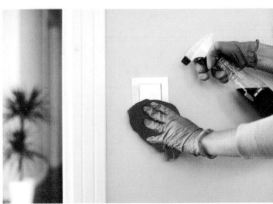

Basic Organizing Checklist for Any Room

Fancy, expensive systems can sometimes make organizing your space feel overwhelming. But it can also be really simple—these basic principles will guide you through sorting out any situation:

- **Store like with like.** It's easier to find and access objects when they're together. Need a mug? They're all on the shelf to the left of the coffee maker, always, end of story.
- **Sort by category.** In the library, they don't just stick any book on any shelf. There's a system. Your own bookshelves don't have to be Dewey decimaled, but keeping all your mysteries (or sweaters, or condiments, etc.) together makes them easier to find.
- **Use vertical space.** Especially in small homes, think tall shelving units, hanging baskets, the top of the fridge, and so on.
- **Incorporate storage into furniture wherever possible.** If all else is equal, choose the side table with drawers over the one without.
- **Prioritize your belongings.** The more you use something, the more front and center its place in your home should be. Less frequently used items can go in less accessible spaces.

Give Everything a Home

Part of being an adult and organizing your space is to know where everything you own lives in your house. When you need some glue, that green scarf, or your passport, you should be able to name its location.

- If you can never find your scissors, that's a sign that their current storage space isn't working out.
- If every surface in your apartment always has a coin or two lying on it, that's a clue that you need to designate a coin jar.
- If you own a thing you just can't figure out where to store, consider whether it really has a place in your current life. Perhaps it should be decluttered.

Avoid These Organizing Mistakes

Save yourself a bunch of trouble by avoiding these organizing don'ts:

- Don't purchase organizing products without measuring. Even a ¼-inch misjudgment can mean your new organizing system is useless.
- Don't feel compelled to buy those nestled sets of organizers in small, medium, and large. They look cute in stores, but IRL, at least one of each set usually turns out to be highly impractical.
- Don't pack as much as you can into every space. Even if it's very organized, a closet that looks like a game of Tetris is not practical. One exception: long-term storage you won't need to access for years.
- Don't keep everything because, hey, you have the space for it. Never decluttering will, over the years, lead to an organization nightmare.

4 Reasons You Might Struggle to Get Organized

If your belongings keep getting out of hand, it's likely due to one of the following reasons:

1. You have too. Much. Stuff. While it's technically *possible* to keep zillions of objects organized, it's also a full-time job; employees of grocery stores, museums, and warehouses get paid for it.

2. You *are* decluttering, but you're acquiring new stuff just as fast. Tackle this habit (whether it's a shopping problem or a free sidewalk furniture addiction) first.

3. Your organizing systems aren't personalized. Like diet and workout plans, what works miracles for some can be useless for others. Redesign your routines working with, not against, your natural tendencies.

4. You have a legit need for more storage space than your home provides. Solutions include renting a storage unit, adding outdoor storage, or asking a friend to stash your stuff in their unused storage space.

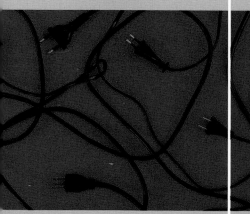

14 Items to Get Rid of Now

If you don't have any particularly cluttered or disorganized areas in your home, but you still feel like you own a lot of stuff you never touch, try decluttering not by room but by type of object. Here are some common culprits:

1. Nonworking pens

2. Old papers or mail

3. Magazines

4. Books, CDs, and DVDs you won't read, listen to, or watch again (or prefer to own a digital copy)

5. Samples of makeup and beauty products

6. Expired or unused medications, vitamins, and bath products

7. Uncomfortable footwear

8. Broken items you're not going to fix

9. Unused or unusable cables, chargers, and plugs

10. Objects from a "previous life," e.g., branded shirts from an old job

11. Expensive items you feel guilty about purchasing and never using

12. Gimmicky gadgets you only used once

13. Kitchen tools you don't need

14. Unnecessary duplicates (of anything)

Less Clutter Means Less Cleaning

You might notice an emphasis on decluttering and owning less throughout this book. That's because owning the wrong stuff makes life more complicated, and owning the right stuff makes life easier. So decluttering, i.e., yeeting, the items you don't need, use, or even like is often the simplest way to start getting your life together.

This is true in all kinds of ways, but to focus on cleaning, if you don't bring home random things, you don't have to clean them. You don't have to find a place for them. You'll never buy more things to go with them, or place on top of them, which you will then have to dust. You see where this is going, right?

If that doesn't make sense, imagine cleaning an empty apartment. Now imagine cleaning the same apartment but it's full of furniture, electronics, and knickknacks. Yeah.

Know How Often to Clean

Acquiring the life skill of knowing how often to clean depends a lot on your situation. How many people do you live with? Are there kids and pets? How often are you home? Do your daily habits and hobbies naturally create chaos? Does the outdoors (insects, sand, mud) always find its way inside? Do you own a ton of stuff or a little?

Generally, you'll do fine if you fully clean areas like bathrooms and kitchens once a week, mopping up spills and quickly wiping surfaces in between. Infrequently used spaces can usually go for 2 weeks, as long as you generally clean up after yourself and keep things tidy.

To determine your personalized routine, start by cleaning every week. Then assess whether this feels like too much or not enough. If some spaces can go longer than a week, great; if some need attention more frequently, clean them more often than once a week.

The Biggest Organizing Don't

Usually, when we get the urge to organize our entire life, the first thing we do is go shopping. Because you can't get organized without buying some kind of storage system, or at least a bunch of plastic containers...right?

Wrong. In fact, this is the quickest way to end up with an expensive and bulky new bunch of clutter.

When you're ready to organize, step one should be decluttering; there's no need to organize what you don't own. Step two is assessing what's left. Once you know exactly what you own and how much space it takes up (you might literally need to measure here), then you can look into what style and size of shelves or bins you need to store it.

And maybe you'll end up decluttering so much you'll discover you don't need any new storage at all!

Deal with Major Types of Clutter

Clutter can keep your life from feeling clean and organized. If you have too much stuff, it can help to recognize the common mental patterns that keep us from parting with unused belongings.

- If it's **sentimental clutter**—like childhood toys—consider taking a photograph to preserve your memories or saving one representative item from the collection.

- With **aspirational clutter**—like abandoned exercise equipment—the solution is honesty. Accept where you are today, and don't let that former fantasy version of yourself control your current actions.

- To release **other people's clutter**—like presents or inherited objects—put your own needs first. Give yourself the gift of passing these objects on.

- To eliminate **bargain clutter**—made up of anything free, on sale, or otherwise "too good to pass up"—work on shifting your perspective. You know what's also a great deal? Not being overloaded with junk.

- If you have **guilt clutter**—feeling bad about wasting perfectly good things—do good by donating them to someone in need or selling them and putting the cash to good use.

20 Areas to Declutter Now

Feeling the need to get rid of unused stuff but don't know where to begin? Run through this checklist of places where clutter often assembles, and start with whatever makes you feel seen:

- Clothes closet
- Clothes dresser/bureau
- Hutch/dining room storage
- Front closet, entryway, and/or mudroom
- Kitchen cabinets
- Kitchen counters
- Linen closet
- Attic
- Basement
- Pantry
- Refrigerator and freezer
- Purses, bags, and luggage
- Paper files
- Dining table, coffee table, and/or side or console tables
- Bookshelves
- That box of stuff from your childhood you were going to "go through later"
- Bathroom cupboards, drawers, and/or closets
- Underbed storage
- Bedside tables
- Outdoor storage areas

Stock Up the Smart Way

Super organized people rarely find themselves completely out of, say, paper towels. That's because they think ahead and stock up on necessities. You, too, can do this by buying bigger quantities of nonperishable items you buy often and go through quickly. If you don't have space for storing extras, set up a system, like recurring deliveries, to purchase smaller quantities of those necessities more regularly. However, there are some don'ts:

- Don't buy too much of anything with an expiration date you won't meet.
- Don't buy an unfamiliar product because a twenty-four-pack of it is a great deal.
- Don't buy a boatload of anything that represents an aspiration rather than a current reality, e.g., a giant tub of protein powder for that fantasy version of yourself who drinks smoothies three times a day.

Manage Your Paper

Despite the ubiquity of cloud storage, almost all of us have certain hard copies for one reason or another. Here's how to manage paper files as painlessly as possible. First, research the rules for whatever documents you're dealing with. Some can safely be shredded after a specific period of time; some you'll need to store, though not necessarily in dead tree form; and some you'll be required to physically hold on to. Others (like appliance manuals) will be readily available online.

Next, sort papers by category. Shred, scan, or file as needed. To make future filing go smoothly, label folders and boxes. You don't need a filing cabinet, but store all papers together using a system that works for what you have.

Finally, stay on top of it. It's easier to organize a few pieces of paper than the Leaning Tower of Filing.

Small Toys, Meet Bins

Children and animals should come with shelving units because they both require lots of stuff. But their stuff is, for the most part, easier to manage than grown-up stuff. For toys, especially, there's no need to be particularly neat: Just toss everything into a large basket or bin—even better if it's an attractive one that matches your decor. And if the little playful ones don't need to be able to access the toys themselves, you can hide all that colorful plastic in a piece of furniture with built-in storage, like a trunk-style coffee table.

Put Things Away Right Away

Organizing your house usually looks like developing a lot of little habits. One of these is taking care of the parade of stuff marching into your home—be it mail, packages, or shopping bags. The faster you deal with this stuff, the less it hangs around becoming clutter. So when you walk in the door, don't just drop everything and chill. Open your mail, flatten those boxes for recycling, and put the groceries away.

Stash Away Off-Season Items

Anything you can't use for at least 3 months at a time is something you should consider putting well out of sight when it's not needed. The most obvious examples are clothes (e.g., heavy sweaters) and season-specific equipment or decor (e.g., skis and holiday decorations). The main benefit of this method is that the unused items won't crowd your main storage spaces during their off-season. Another major plus: It helps you recognize clutter. If summer ends and you realize you never wore one of your bathing suits, then you know it's time to let it go.

Make Inexpensive Organizers Look Classy

Perhaps surprisingly, it's pretty easy to get organized on a budget. Assuming you really need new bins and boxes, here's how to make affordable ones look stylish:

- **Stick to neutrals.** Using colors like black, white, or tan—and choosing organizers in only one or two of these colors—will streamline and upscale the look of your storage.
- **Embrace uniformity.** Uniqueness is awesome—unless you're a storage product, in which case it's usually better to blend in. Think of how aesthetically pleasing a row of identical glass Mason jars looks.
- **Choose natural materials.** The aforementioned glass jars, paper or wood boxes, straw baskets, and metal bins are all inexpensive and tasteful options.
- **Use clear organizers (carefully).** Transparent storage looks sophisticated when the item being stored is attractive in itself. (Think dry pasta or sleek lipstick cases.) But when the objects you're storing are less cute, forget the see-through stuff and stash it away in something opaque.

Get These Basic Cleaning Supplies

If you're starting from scratch (in a new place or with a new cleaning habit), here's what you need for your cleaning starter pack:

- Liquid all-purpose cleanser in a spray bottle
- Dish soap
- Sponges
- Hand soap
- A wet/dry mop, plus the matching wet and dry cloths (or DIY with rags sprayed with all-purpose cleanser)
- A vacuum cleaner (a little handheld one is fine at first)
- Rubber gloves
- Cloth rags and/or paper towels
- Disinfectant spray or wipes
- A toilet brush

Organize Your Closet

It feels like a formidable task, but organizing your closet (see also: dresser drawers, etc.) is so worth it. It'll be easier and quicker to find and access everything you need. Follow these tips:

- Before you start, remove all your clothes so you can see the big wardrobe picture.
- Declutter. There's no use organizing clothes you don't wear. (Clean the closet and discard unused or broken hangers while you're at it.)
- Consider storing off-season clothes elsewhere, or at least at the back of the closet.
- Place clothes in the closet divided by category. Clothing type (e.g., dresses, tops) and color are typical categories, but use whatever helps you find what you need.
- If you have very different wardrobes for work, outdoor activities, dressy events, and so on, create sections for these categories too, so you won't have to wade through ten fleece hoodies to find your office cardigan.

Overcome Decluttering Anxiety

If you really struggle to get rid of things you don't need anymore, try these remedies:

- If you're good at cleaning but not so good at organizing, make a point to discard one object from each room you clean.
- If decluttering feels hard because it represents letting go of a former hobby or a clothing size you'll never see again, make the decision—and take action—to get rid of that stuff *now*. If something changes in the future, you can try to acquire updated items then. It actually feels liberating and often inspires you to keep going.
- If you're paralyzed with indecision about organizing lots of little things, just declutter one big thing. Finally get rid of the broken recliner or ugly armoire that takes up half the darn room.
- If you doubt your judgment, take a preliminary step: Put everything you're tempted to declutter in boxes in one closet. In 2 or 3 months, if you haven't missed the items, you can feel safe to let them go.

Make Your Own
EASY, NATURAL
Home Cleaning Products

VINEGAR

Baking Soda

You'll feel like a DIY expert when you whip up your very own collection of cleaners.

1. Multipurpose cleanser: Into a spray bottle, pour 2 cups white vinegar, 2 cups water, a few drops lavender essential oil, and a few drops lemon essential oil. Shake to mix.

2. Bathroom cleanser: Into a spray bottle, pour 1 cup rubbing alcohol, 1 cup white vinegar, $1\frac{1}{2}$ cups distilled water, and a few drops of any essential oil you like. Stir mixture.

3. Toilet cleaner: Into a lidded bottle, pour 1 cup baking soda, 1 cup pure castile soap, 2 cups distilled water, and a few drops of your favorite essential oil. Shake. To use, pour into bowl and let slt for 15 minutes before scrubbing with a brush, then flush.

4. Glass cleaner: Into a spray bottle, pour $1\frac{1}{2}$ cups rubbing alcohol, $1\frac{1}{2}$ cups distilled water, and $1\frac{1}{2}$ tablespoons white vinegar, then shake.

5. Floor cleaner: Fill a lidded bottle with pure castile soap. Add a few drops pine, tea tree, or lemon essential oil. Add a small amount into a bucket of water, then mop.

And FYI:
- Avoid using acid-based cleaners (these include anything with vinegar or citrus, and many products formulated for cleaning tile or metal) on marble, limestone, or travertine.
- Use a funnel to make pouring ingredients mess-free.
- Buy distilled water in any grocery or drugstore.

6 Secrets of Clean and Organized People

If you've ever wondered how they do it, here's how. And you can do it too.

1. They make the process enjoyable, whether it's listening to podcasts or embracing the meditative aspect of brainless tasks.

2. They prioritize the perks. Vacuuming isn't thrilling, but naturally neat people love (or at least appreciate) a vacuumed rug.

3. They clean preventatively. Sure, they'll wipe up spills and do occasional deep-cleanings. But mostly, they do frequent light tasks to avoid doing heavy-duty ones later.

4. They're observant. Tidy people always see that sock lying on the floor. And it low-key (or high-key) bugs them.

5. They feel their space reflects them. Cleaning and tidying, therefore, is kind of like washing their face: just part of feeling presentable.

6. They're future-oriented. Fun as it is to live in the moment, clean and tidy types know that eventually they'll have to clean that fun up. They prefer to do it sooner (the night of the party) rather than foisting the task onto their future selves.

Embrace Your Junk Drawers

Having a junk drawer seems to be a natural consequence of being a human with belongings. And, believe it or not, junk drawers can actually be a functional part of an organized home (provided they don't expand into junk rooms).

A junk drawer should not contain literal junk, which belongs in the trash, or things you never use, which should be decluttered. And it shouldn't be a mess; keep it orderly using small containers or the type of divider you'd see in a cutlery drawer.

What a junk drawer *should* be is a catchall for small objects you do need but don't have another logical place to store. It should be the obvious answer to the question "Where's that thingamabob?"

Keep Your Floors Clean

Entire shelves of specialized products are sold for every imaginable floor-cleaning need, but for light cleaning of most floors, vacuuming to remove dust and using a damp mop on everyday dirt is fine. Here are some simple cleaning solutions for specific surfaces:

- Clean **laminate** floors with a damp mop and a water and white vinegar mixture.
- For **ceramic, linoleum, and vinyl** tiles, a mild detergent should work well.
- **Wood** floors should be swept or vacuumed often to pick up dust and washed with a damp mop. Avoid using harsh cleansers or too much water on wood floors.

When dealing with serious stains or delicate flooring, do more research on your surface (or check the manufacturer's instructions of the cleaning product) before jumping in with any old cleanser.

Try These Fridge & Freezer Organization Hacks

Messy fridge? Clear plastic organizers are your friend. And you don't have to use ones intended for food storage! Feel free to get creative with differently shaped containers sold as makeup, office, or shower organizers. For example:

- Use long, slim rectangular bins to corral bottles of sparkling water.
- Stick a little suction-backed organizer to a fridge wall for holding small snacks, like string cheese.
- Place a turntable on a refrigerator shelf to eliminate the stuck-at-the-back-of-the-fridge problem. It will provide instant easy access to single-serve yogurts, smaller condiment jars, or little packets of any food.
- Stock cylindrical, lidded containers with fresh snacks, like washed blueberries and baby carrots.
- Use transparent magazine holders as dividers in your freezer to keep bags of frozen vegetables in place.
- And a nonplastic bonus hack: Repurpose an empty egg carton bottom to hold upside-down bottles of ketchups and salad dressings.

Organize Your Pantry and Kitchen Cabinets

Every so often, it's a good idea to thoroughly reassess your food storage areas. Here's a game plan:

- Take everything out of the cabinet and/or pantry.
- Toss empty containers, stale food, and expired items. Consolidate duplicates when possible.

- Clean the inside of the cabinets. (For a quick DIY cleaner, mix equal parts water and white vinegar plus a few strips of orange peel.)
- If desired, place nonperishable foods into clearly labeled glass jars. The jars aren't just for looks; they also keep critters out of your food, reduce packaging waste, and allow you to see how much of the item you have on hand.
- Put everything away, with frequently used items front and center and extras and rare ingredients higher up. Customize your storage by adjusting the placement of your shelves if possible and choosing organizers that fit your needs. Tiered inserts help you see and access small items, like spice jars, while narrow plastic boxes keep oils from dripping onto shelves.

Maximize Space in a Small Kitchen

In what a real estate listing might call a "cozy kitchen," you need to make the most of the space you've got. Try these tips:

- Use a pegboard to hang pots and pans (or anything that will fit) on a wall.
- Hang the best of your canvas shopping bags on your kitchen doorknob and store all your other reusable bags (or plastic shopping bags you want to reuse) inside it.
- Use the dead zones of a tiny kitchen for storage by hanging baskets from the ceiling and installing hooks or small floating shelves on awkward wall spaces.
- Get the most out of unused shelf space with organizers that hang below shelves.
- Alternate wine glasses upside down and right side up to save space.

- Store lids neatly using a small dish rack, and stack their matching containers nearby.
- Optimize the space under the sink with a shelf insert that turns one level into two.

CHAPTER 2

Home Decor & Improvement

OVERCOME YOUR FEAR OF TOOLS

Being in charge of your own living space is a double-edged sword. (Or perhaps a double-edged chisel.) You can arrange and decorate the way you want to, but you have to fix things when they go wrong.

This chapter is packed with ideas for **decorating** and basic **home repair skills**—the kinds of things you might think you "should" know already. (Don't worry if you don't!) There are also plenty of fun hacks to help you choose a paint color and roll it on those walls yourself.

Patch Up Holes

Filling unsightly holes left by old nails in your walls is one of the easiest—and most oddly satisfying—quick home fixes. First, clean away any peeling paint. Then grab a small tub of spackling paste and a putty knife. Carefully apply the product—you just need a little!—so it fills the hole. Scrape away excess spackle as you go. Let dry and repeat if needed.

Get Yourself a Toolbox

If you don't have a toolbox yet, it's time to get one. Not only will it keep all your home repair tools together and safe in one convenient and portable case; it will also make you feel like an adult who has their life together. (Or at least the DIY project piece of your life.)

Fix Wobbly Furniture

If a chair or table is unstable, even it out with stick-on pads made to protect flooring. (Double up if one isn't enough.) Or cut an appropriately sized slice off a wine cork and glue it to the short leg.

Remove Wall-to-Wall Carpet

The nastier an old carpet is, the more satisfying it is to rip it up and throw it away. Here's how to free your floors:

- Wearing work gloves and a mask, find a loose corner of carpet and tug. (Pliers are handy here.) If your carpet is stuck fast, use a utility knife to pry up a corner or edge.
- If the room is very small, you may be able to pull it away easily. For a larger carpet, cut into strips with a utility knife and roll up each strip as you remove it.
- If there's padding under the carpet, remove this the same way.
- Next, remove the tack strips around the perimeter of the room using a pry bar and hammer.
- Finally, search the floor carefully for leftover nails and staples. Pull them up with a claw hammer and/or carpet staple remover.

Now you'll have to assess and deal with the floor underneath...that might be a whole new project. But at least it's not a carpet!

Use a Stud Finder

Yeah, yeah, insert joke about dating apps here. If you're hanging a shelf or anything heavier than a small picture frame, you'll probably need to locate the "studs" (or vertical pieces of wood on which your drywall is hung). (That's because drywall or plaster won't support heavy items nailed or screwed into it, and your shelf might crash to the floor.) Stud finders use magnets or electricity to detect studs within your walls. They're very afford-able and can be found at any hardware store or wherever you usually buy household goods and gadgets in person or online. There are also more accurate—and more expensive—models that use radar.

Top Tools for Basic Home Repairs

You know you're an adult when you want to go on a shopping spree at the hardware store. Here's what to grab if you're just starting out with home repairs and DIY projects:

- A hammer
- Screwdrivers (at least one flathead and one Phillips)
- A cordless electric drill
- A set of drill bits
- Pliers; consider getting a set, as different types come in handy
- A wrench or two in different sizes
- A tube of strong, quick-drying glue
- A sturdy retractable measuring tape
- A level, aka a bubble level (there are also smartphone level apps if you prefer)
- Nails, in a variety of shapes and sizes
- Screws, in a variety of shapes and sizes
- A utility knife
- A ladder and/or step stool
- A pry bar

Know Your Hammer Parts

Here's a beginner tip that will blow your new-to-DIY mind: You know the other side of the hammer, that sort of two-pronged curved part that's totally useless for hammering in nails? It's for pulling nails out. Just slide the stuck nail between the two metal pieces, press down in the direction the hammer curves, and pull the nail out practically effortlessly.

(BTW, hammers with this feature are called claw hammers, and they're what you should get if you're buying a hammer for the first time.)

Learn These Two Screwdriver Types

You know when you're reading instructions for, say, assembling flat-pack furniture, and they require a specific type of screwdriver, and you're like, isn't the world difficult enough?

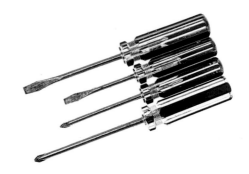

The most common types are **flathead** and **Phillips** screwdrivers. You'll need to own one of each before you start doing basic DIY projects. Flatheads have a tip that's, well, flat, while Phillips have a pointed tip that resembles a plus sign shape. These correspond with the most common screwheads. (There are other kinds, but you probably won't have to use them for everyday repairs.)

Repair Loose Tiles

If your entire tile floor is cracked and crumbling, that's going to be either a major DIY undertaking or a job for a pro. But if just a few floor tiles have come loose, you can probably reattach them yourself with commercially sold tile adhesive. At least, it won't hurt your floor or your wallet to try.

Replace Appliance Light Bulbs

Let's say one day you open your fridge and it's unusually dark and ominous in there. You think the appliance is dead and wonder how you're going to eat all that cheese. But...wait a second. Before you panic, check the light bulb. We take the fridge light for granted to the point that we simply forget it's there, but you can easily change it yourself just like any other light bulb. Check the old bulb to be sure you buy a new one with the correct wattage. And *then* calmly eat some cheese.

Personalize Furniture

If you're ever drawn to a piece of furniture but are unsure about its color or hardware, don't automatically pass it by. It might be worth the effort to slap a few coats of paint on it or replace its knobs and pulls. These are really simple and often inexpensive ways to add your own style to any piece of furniture, and they can make a major difference in the look and feel of your space.

Decorate Sustainably, for Free

Even if your decorating budget is approximately $0.00, you can still give your space a beautiful personal touch—with nature! Whenever you're in the great outdoors, scan your surroundings for unusual seashells, flowers (fresh and dried), driftwood, sea glass, pretty leaves, or anything that catches your eye. These organic items can be showcased in all sorts of creative ways, and they're ideal for anyone who likes to celebrate the seasons with home decor.

Plus, when you want to change it up, there's no guilt or complex decluttering process: Just return your decorations to the wilderness.

Understanding Color Palettes

If you're feeling like your decor looks all over the place, consider your colors. One foolproof way to keep your home looking neat and stylish is to keep everything within the same color palette. It means using, say, soft sage greens alongside tans and creams. Or sticking (mostly) to a blue and white theme. By limiting your colors, you eliminate visual distractions and help your home feel more "mature domicile" and less "messy dorm room." Plus, it makes shopping way less overwhelming!

Hang It Up

Very light items (like sheets of paper and small ornaments) don't require a drill or screws. They can be hung on the wall with just a nail. As a bonus, this technique can also help create a natural, minimalistic look (if you're into that). Hang the decorative items directly on the nails, or secure each one with a small binder clip and flip one arm up to hang that from the nail.

Another easy hanging method is to use sticky-backed hooks. These can hold anything from bags to brooms to framed paintings, and if you double—or quadruple—up, they can support more weight than you might imagine.

Try a Small Amount of Wallpaper

If you love the idea of wallpaper but don't want to make the leap to a full floral-covered living room, pick a small area of your wall that's naturally separated (e.g., the triangle of wall formed by a staircase) and apply a stick-on paper. It's the simplest way to add a touch of visual interest without the major design or time commitment.

Replace Light Switch Covers

Is your room looking vaguely old and tired? Try replacing dingy-looking light switch and outlet plates to instantly perk it up. Just going from discolored white plates to fresh new ones will make everything look cleaner, and introducing slightly fancier silver- or brass-toned plates can add a new, distinctive look to a space. It's like a good, subtle haircut: The room will look noticeably better, but no one will know why.

Paint Finishes 101

Paint comes in a variety of finishes, or sheens. Here's what they mean:

- **Flat or matte:** This finish doesn't reflect light. It's a good choice for walls that aren't perfectly smooth. It's easy to touch up but can be damaged by cleansers.
- **Eggshell:** Slightly more durable than matte paint, this finish has the slightest shine, like, well, an eggshell.
- **High gloss:** As shiny as it gets, this finish is also used for trim, such as door and window frames.

- **Semigloss:** Sleek and shiny, it's great for trim, as well as bathrooms and other areas where walls can come in contact with water.
- **Satin:** Neither flat nor shiny, this popular pearlescent finish looks lustrous, but it can also be tricky to apply on imperfect walls.

5 Small-Space Decor Tips

Many decor rules are universal, but small spaces do have their own needs. If your home is...cozy, remember these:

1. Double up. In addition to combining furniture with storage, try to find other pieces with multiple functions. There's a reason so many small spaces contain a couch that's also a bed.

2. Cut clutter ruthlessly. It's a helpful tip for anyone, but for those living in tiny houses or one-room apartments, it's a must.

3. Use a "less is more" philosophy. Decorations you might be able to get away with in a spacious room can easily overwhelm a smaller one. This is actually a plus: You can achieve a simple or cozy feel with less effort.

4. Make necessities the statement piece. A beautiful blanket can go far when you don't have room for any other bedroom decor.

5. Use everyday objects as artworks. Put your prettiest bowls out on display, or hang a vintage straw hat on your bedpost.

Upgrade Your Home Decor from Immature to Sophisticated

If your space feels more "teen" than "functional adult," here are some simple ways you can take your decor from minor to mature:

- **A very large mirror.** One big enough to see your entire outfit without jumping up and down.

- **A large natural material rug.** Think sisal or jute. If you're not sure how to pronounce it, it's a grown-up rug.

- **A set of matching mugs.** No more random souvenirs with silly phrases on them.

- **Refillable glass bottles** (instead of the plastic ones from the drugstore) for hand soap by the sink.

- **An L-shaped, U-shaped, or chaise sectional.** A couch with room for more than one person to relax on it.

- **A few houseplants** that are a) potted nicely, not in flimsy plastic pots from the garden store; and b) alive.

- **Quality fabrics.** Anything made of cloth, from bedsheets to bath towels to oven mitts, is either giving luxe or low-rent vibes. It's your choice.

Take Your Time

Some things can't be forced, and one of these is making a house look homey. After moving into a new house or apartment, give yourself plenty of time to find your way in decorating. Get the essentials first (you need some kind of bedding and dinnerware ASAP), but don't rush to buy every throw pillow and painting at once. Live in the space for a while and then decide what you want.

Use Fake Plants in a Classy Way

Cheating is wrong...except when it means decorating with fake plants. But that doesn't mean sticking pots of plastic petunias all over your space. Instead, consider using lengths of faux ivy and other leafy vines to create a curtain separating two rooms, or draping them over the edge of an otherwise basic bookshelf, or hanging them in place of a headboard. While phony flowers can look dated and sad, well-made leaf look-alikes can brighten up a space in a modern way.

Surprisingly Easy DIYs DIY

Even if you're new to home repair, there are some tasks you can do yourself if you have a little time and the willingness to follow directions. Try these before paying someone to do them for you:

• Replace a doorknob (if it's a standard size, which some older doors may not have).

• Install blinds and shades.

• Hang curtains and curtain rods.

• Spray-paint metal furniture or hardware.

• Replace toilet seats and lids.

• Paint a room or a piece of furniture.

• Assemble flat-packed furniture. (Though if the piece is very large, you might need a partner.)

Know When to Call a Pro

When a home thing goes haywire, it can be hard to judge whether you should call for help. There's so much DIY advice floating around online these days, you might think you should attempt everything yourself. But unless you're an expert already, that's not always the safest idea. Here's how to know when to call a professional:

- When buying the tools would cost as much as having the job done professionally. (Especially if it's something that's a one-time task.)
- When it involves plumbing, electric, HVAC, or anything else people go to special training programs and get licensed for.
- When asbestos or hazmat or any dangerous material is involved.
- When the fix requires dangerous climbing.
- When getting it wrong would make it much worse, or if what you're planning is irreversible.
- When the broken part is antiquated, nonstandard, or niche, requiring specific experience you won't get from the Internet.

No Heat?
Check the Thermostat Batteries

If you wake up one cold morning to find your heat has stopped heating, don't immediately assume something's gone check-your-bank-balance level wrong. Before you call the professionals, check your thermostat. It could simply need a new battery.

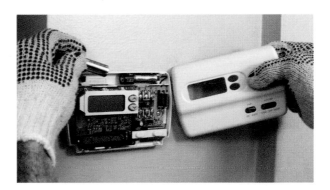

Clogs, Toilet Edition

A clogged toilet probably doesn't need a plumber; it just needs a plunger. If plunging doesn't solve the problem, then you should call a plumber (or your landlord or management company, if you rent) because the problem might be bigger than just a clog. If you've never used a plunger, it's easy—just hold the end of the handle, press the rubber bottom against the bowl as firmly as you can (think suction cup) and push down on the handle, then lift up, and repeat until the clog is dislodged.

Open a Stuck Window

If you can't get your window open, step one is to check the lock. (This is one of those *duh* moments, like when you try to make a smoothie without realizing your blender isn't plugged in.) If it's in the unlocked position, the frame may have swelled in the heat or been painted shut at some point. Try tapping gently but firmly all around the lower sash (i.e., the wooden frame around the lower windowpanes that should slide up and down) with a hammer to loosen it. Another trick is to cut through paint drips with a utility knife.

Shut Out the Cold

If you always feel like a human icicle in winter, try this before cranking up the heat and putting on all your coats at once. Install some peel-and-stick weather stripping around your doors and windows. It's cheap and easy to do by yourself, and it will shut out some of that arctic air. Plus, it can help reduce your energy bills!

Skip the Drip. Drip. Drip.

Sometimes, a constantly dripping faucet is a sign of a larger problem, but most of the time, your sink just needs a new washer. Grab one at a hardware store and try to replace it (just follow the directions on the package) before calling for help.

Prevent Problems Around the House

In addition to knowing how to fix stuff, it's always good to know how to avoid problems to begin with. Because the easiest home repairs...are the ones you never have to make.

- Don't flush wipes or any other sanitary products aside from toilet paper down the toilet.
- Know the signs of mice and catch them before they stage a full-on invasion. These include chewed-up wood, food packaging, or other items; droppings; and unsettling "scratch scratch" noises in the walls.
- Never use electronics with frayed or damaged cords. It can start a fire that quickly gets out of hand.
- Place felt protectors on chair and table legs to prevent scratches to your floors.
- Use sliders when moving heavy furniture, both to protect floors and also to make it easier on your back.
- Know where to find the shutoff switches for your home's water, gas, and electricity, as well as how to shut off sinks and toilets individually.

5 Frugal (& Simple) Decor Tips

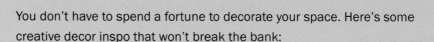

You don't have to spend a fortune to decorate your space. Here's some creative decor inspo that won't break the bank:

1. Thrift store paintings themselves can be questionable, but the frames they come in can be cool—and you're getting them at a fraction of the price. Grab one, then replace the painting with something more modern—like pretty paper or a cool T-shirt.

2. Line the back of your plain bookshelf with leftover wallpaper so a pop of pattern shows behind the books.

3. Use found furniture for the "wrong" purpose, e.g., turn a bar cart into a bedside table.

4. Salvage an old, damaged item by beating it up some more—with sandpaper, a hammer, or whatever works—to create a distressed vintage piece.

5. Reuse high-quality cardboard boxes to store towels or other household items. Cover the outside with rope or nice paper and line the inside with fabric.

Other Uses for Caulk

Caulk isn't just helpful for sealing your bathtub: It can also be used to cover little imperfections throughout your home, such as filling gaps in molding or around shelves in cabinets. To keep your tube of caulk from drying out between uses, stick a screw in the nozzle.

Try These Lovely (and Super Easy) Decorating Ideas

Sometimes decorating can seem like it requires a lot of effort. And who has time to dedicate their lives to making everything look perfect? But there is another way: the lazy way. For example:

- Hang your favorite bags or pretty sachets on doorknobs.
- Display your best-looking books, placing a few large volumes on the coffee table and a little collection of beautiful cookbooks in the kitchen.
- How genius are floor pillows? Lighter and easier to bring home than chairs, they also give you an excuse to eat dinner while lounging on the floor like it's ancient times.
- Fill large glass jars with interesting collections (like shells or marbles).
- Don't want to deal with hanging mirrors or framed art? Don't bother. Lean large pieces against walls for a bohemian look. Forget bookcases too: Stacks of books will give your space that absent-minded intellectual atmosphere.

Make Recycling Less Ugly

If you keep your recycling indoors before taking it out on pickup day, you don't need to "decorate" your kitchen with one of those ubiquitous blue bins. Instead, stash empty bottles and boxes in a nice laundry hamper or woven basket to add a bit of class to your kitchen, then just transfer your recycling to the municipal bin.

Assessing the Scale of Your Space

Some spaces just look *off*. We've all seen living rooms uncomfortably full of bulky furniture or waited awkwardly in a cavernous foyer with just a tiny table in it. What's going on here is that the scale is off. Larger spaces (vertical as well as horizontal) need larger furniture, while smaller ones require smaller pieces. These tips can also help:

- Avoid scale fails by measuring first: Don't just guess how many inches a pendant lamp should drop from the ceiling.
- Before you buy furniture, mark its outline on the floor with tape. A 100-inch-wide couch will fit in a 110-inch-wide room, but the tape will help you see whether that translates to cozy or cramped.
- Another tip: Take photos of your rooms from different angles. It's kind of like seeing a pic of yourself in those pants you thought looked cool.
- Finally, don't feel you need to fill every inch of a room; think more about balancing empty space with proportional pieces.

Elevate Your Necessities

When you want your home to look just slightly more polished, it really *is* the little things that count. The next time you're shopping for mundane necessities, choose the slightly fancier version. Boring things like tissue boxes, hand soaps, and shower curtains all come in thousands of different colors and patterns as well as seasonal styles. Choosing the special ones over their basic counterparts just makes your home look more intentional, with almost no added effort.

Play with Patterns

If you're nervous about trying out patterns in your home decor, follow these guidelines to avoid polka-dot regret:

- Start with easily replaceable items. Floral throw pillow? Yay! Floral wallpaper? Maybe no.

- Coordinate patterns with your overall color palette. Use them to incorporate different shades of the same color or to introduce pops of an accent color.

- Stick to less intimidating patterns, like stripes. (Think classic, timeless, and fresh—not trending.)

- Use bold patterns in small doses. Stair risers are an ideal spot for an intricate print.

- Keep patterns behind closed doors. A bathroom, for example, is the perfect place to install a busy tile floor without letting it influence the look of your entire home.

- To test your love for a very daring print, start with small *and* replaceable items. You can always add more later, but initially try a lacquer tray covered in leopards before stenciling jungle fauna all over your walls.

Look for Storage + Decor Two-for-One Options

As the proliferation of van life and tiny house content shows, everyone loves a sweet little space. But when living small, you have to be smart about storage. The simplest principle of space-saving home decorating? Combine decor and storage whenever possible. When choosing new living room furniture, look for pieces that come with built-in drawers. When personalizing a room, find a way to make it practical; for example, if you love the look of antique crates, use them to store extra blankets.

How to
PAINT A ROOM

Painting is time-consuming, but in most cases, it's easy to do yourself. It's also hands down one of the best low(ish)-cost ways to make a huge difference in how your home looks and feels.

1. Remove any furniture or other items from the room if possible. If not, move them to the center of the room and cover them with old sheets or drop cloths.

2. Clean and dust the walls and ceiling.

3. Remove outlet and light switch plate covers, then tape over outlets to shield them from drips.

4. Lay drop cloths on the floor.

5. Remove any nails and spackle small holes to prep. (Sand and prime over spackled areas if necessary.)

6. Open and stir your paint. Pour paint into a small container.

7. Painter's tape on trim and baseboards is optional; if you use it, make sure it's carefully applied so paint doesn't seep through.

8. Start by "cutting in" corners and edges with an angled brush (meaning, slowly paint the edges first). Begin with the ceiling cut, then the corners, then the baseboards. Use smooth strokes and feather the edges so the paint doesn't run.

9. While cut-in paint is still slightly wet, begin painting with small amounts of paint on your roller. Start at the top and work down.

10. Fully cover the wall once before rolling over it a second time (without adding more paint) to smooth it. Go slowly and avoid over-saturating your roller or pressing too hard. Continue until you're done.

11. After the paint dries, add a second coat if necessary.

12. Carefully remove any tape and drop cloths.

13. Clean brushes and rollers under running water. This can take quite a while, and it's messy, so don't do it in your nicest sink. (If you're not going to reuse the roller again soon, you might want to just toss it instead.) Reshape brushes before they dry.

Don't Ignore Your Lighting

Your choice of light fixtures can have an outsize impact on a space. Think of a plain white room. Now imagine an industrial metal light hanging from the ceiling—or an elaborate glittering chandelier—or a funky modern fixture that looks like it came from space. That room would feel very different with each light option, right?

Even if you can't change what's on the ceiling, you can add floor lamps or table lamps to change up the style of your space. And as you're dealing with lighting, remember that the bulbs you choose can make a room feel warmer, sleeker, or—obviously—brighter. Just pay attention to the wattage limits of the fixture.

4 Unique Sources of Home Decor

Tired of the same old furniture and decor sources? These options are more creative and often more affordable too:

1. Architectural salvage shops: You might pass these by because you're not looking for vintage steel mill machinery or whatever. But they're also good for one-of-a-kind repurposed coffee tables, storage cabinets, and conversation-starting decor pieces.

2. Garden stores and farm markets: They often sell beautiful pots and planters (the kind you can decorate with even if you're not a gardener) as well as unique ceramics, small home accents, and other surprises.

3. Museum shops: They can be a classy source for small decorative items, coffee table books, and high-quality posters and prints.

4. Gift stores: You know, those lovely boutiques where you'd buy a beautiful serving tray as a housewarming gift for someone else? Maybe shop there for yourself once in a while!

How to Thrift Shop

A thrift store, flea market, yard sale, or resale shop can seem at first glance like a pile of, well, junk. But most of the time, if you really look, you can find some gems. Here's how to approach secondhand home furnishing shopping:

- **Make a list.** Don't be thrown off the bookshelf hunt because that flamingo lamp looks so fun.
- **Look out for quality.** Paint color, hardware, and upholstery can be upgraded; you can even repair some broken items. But you'll never make up for shoddy craftsmanship, cheap materials, or serious damage.
- **Think timeless.** If you can imagine something looking as good 50 years ago or 20 years from now, it's a win.

Temporary Decor for Renters

When you're renting, you might have strict rules about what you can and can't change. But there are ways to make your rental your own via simple—and removable—decor ideas:

- **Self-adhesive hooks.** Use these instead of nails or screws to hang anything on the walls.
- **Privacy film.** It doesn't just make glass less see-through; it also changes the whole look of windows and doors.
- **Peel-and-stick anything.** Removeable options can give you new counters, cabinets, or even walls.
- **Throw rugs.** You can't install carpet, but you can cover an unsightly floor with rugs for a whole new style.
- **Tension rods.** These let you hang curtains from any door or window frame and take them down in seconds.

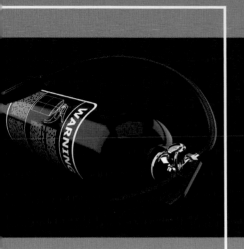

5 Safety Items Every Home Needs

There's nothing more adult than worrying about safety. Here are some gadgets that can give you some peace of mind in this department:

1. Smoke and carbon monoxide detectors: Check local regulations to find out how many are required and where they should be installed, and put it in your calendar to test and/or replace the batteries regularly.

2. A fire extinguisher: Some fires, especially ones that happen in the kitchen, can't be put out with water. (When in doubt, though, always evacuate and call emergency services!)

3. A high-quality flashlight or two: You'll need these in case of a power outage or if you have to check out a dark corner of the basement or attic to deal with a problem. Don't rely on your phone for this: Get a proper battery-operated flashlight.

4. A battery-operated radio: To get updates during, or in the aftermath of, severe storms or other outages.

5. Batteries, in different sizes: Be the hero that has backup batteries—for remotes, flashlights, radios, and so on.

Consider Owning These Extra Tools

Alongside your basic tools, owning a few more useful (and inexpensive!) options can make both decorating and repairing things around your home easier and more fun. Consider adding these versatile items to your toolbox:

- **A staple gun:** You'll never realize how many things you always wanted to *pop* into their place until you get one.
- **A label maker:** From kitchen containers to bathroom shelves to kids' rooms to file folders, label makers give your space a uniform look.
- **A hot glue gun:** They're not just for crafts; you might find yourself using warm glue to do all sorts of little home repairs.
- **A set of old-school "school supplies":** Because rulers, high-quality scissors, and pencils stay useful long after you graduate. Grown-up uses for these include measuring furniture dimensions and drawing straight lines, cutting everything from paper to packing tape to those peel-and-stick tiles, and marking your walls so you don't hang things all wonky.

Light It Up

Night-lights aren't just for kids scared of underbed monsters. They're also perfect for lighting up dark areas that don't have light fixtures or areas you want to stay just slightly illuminated for safety when the sun goes down (e.g., bathrooms or hallways). And you can choose between old-fashioned lamp-style nightlights or sleeker, more modern styles.

A DIY Fix for Slow Drains

Clogged drains are yucky and inconvenient. Commercial products that unclog them are usually effective—but can be pretty harsh. You can make your own drain de-clogger to tackle simple clogs with ingredients you probably already have in your kitchen. Here's how to do it:

1. Remove the drain cap.

2. Mix equal parts baking soda and salt in a bowl.

3. Pour the baking soda mixture down the drain.

4. Pour warm white vinegar down the drain and let sit for a few minutes.

5. Pour boiling water down the drain until it clears.

6. Return the drain cap to its place. Enjoy your newly functioning drain!

Store the mixture of baking soda and salt in an airtight container for next time. Because knowing drains, there will be one.

Measure (At Least) Twice

You've probably heard the phrase "Measure twice, cut once." It's excellent advice, but it doesn't go far enough. Don't just measure things you're about to cut: Measure *everything* you work on in your home. Don't just assume that (for example) two windows right next to each other in the same room have the exact same dimensions.

Free a Shower Clog

Shower drain full of hair? First, ew. Second, here's a very simple hack to unclog it:

1. Get a wire hanger and pair of pliers.

2. Completely unfold the hanger so it's a relatively straight strip.

3. Use the pliers to bend the wire at the end where the hook was and create a handle.

4. At the other end of your wire strip, leaving the corkscrew intact, use the pliers to bend back the tip and form a tiny hook.

5. Insert the wire, hook end first, into your drain. Using the handle, twist the wire clockwise several times.

6. Pull the wire out of the drain along with all the nasty hair that's been in there for longer than you want to think about.

Pad Your Project Timelines

Optimism and motivation are lovely, but when you're starting a home repair project, expect some snags. Plan for it to take much longer than you think. If you do get it done fast, awesome! But if not, you won't be scrambling to reschedule when your "2-day" project actually takes 2 weeks.

Choose the Right Extension Cord

If you ever doubt that life is absurdly complicated, try shopping for an extension cord. Boring as it sounds, it's really important to make sure the cord you buy is the right one for the task.

Cords are labeled as indoor or outdoor use. (Kind of like with cats, outdoor cords will do fine indoors, if you want them there, but indoor cords shouldn't go out.) Also check the length, amperage, and gauge. Length is self-explanatory. Amperage refers to how many amps of power the cord can handle. Gauge will be a number like 12, 14, or 16—the lower the number, the thicker and more powerful the cord. If you're replacing a cord, just find a new one with the same specs. Otherwise, check the user manual of whatever you're plugging in to see what type of cord is compatible. And finally, check the plug and your outlets. Extension cords can have two or three prongs.

How to Hang Something Heavy on Your Wall

To hang a heavier item, first find the right place to drill. This means locating the wall studs. Most studs are 16 inches to 24 inches apart, and you can find them by using an electric or magnetic stud finder.

If that's not possible, you'll need to buy a drywall anchor. Check the packaging to determine the weight capacity of anchors before using. Plastic expansion anchors, used for relatively lighter weights, are often included with items like picture frames. You can also buy these or self-drilling anchors, which hold slightly more weight.

Heavier objects may require a hollow wall anchor, toggle bolts, or Snaptoggle bolt. The installation methods vary, but most anchors require a drill with the correct size bit and a hammer.

To place your object correctly, measure carefully with a ruler and use a level at every step to ensure your lines are straight. Mark the lines on the wall with a pencil. Also, if there are screw holes in the object you want to mount, hold the object in place and trace inside the screw holes so you'll know exactly where to drill.

After drilling your holes, hold the object in place and double-check that it's level. Drill screws in loosely at first so you can adjust if needed.

When the screws are tightened, mount the object to the wall and check again that it's level.

Nailed It!

You know how annoying it is, when you're nailing in a nail or screwing in a screw, to have to hold that nail or screw with one hand as you use your hammer or screwdriver with the other? Next time, try these tricks:

- For **nails**, trace and cut a small X shape in an old mousepad, then cut the pad into a small circle so that the X is in the center. Place the pad against the wall over the spot where the nail goes, and push the nail through the X. The dense material will hold the nail in place while you hammer.

- With **screws**, stick a small, strong magnet on the metal part of the screwdriver, close to the tip. Now fit the screw to the tlp of the screwdriver. It should stay there, attracted by the magnet's pull. Now you can screw it into place without having to hold it.

Reset a Tripped Breaker

If you ever plug in your kettle and space heater at the same time and half the power goes out, congrats: You've tripped a breaker! This is super simple and quick to fix.

First, make sure all lights and appliances are switched off. Then find the service panel (that little metal box on or set into the wall with a pop-open door; it's often located in the basement but can be anywhere). Inside, the breakers may be labeled with the areas of the house they correspond to. If so, look for the room where your power outage happened. That breaker will be flipped in a different direction from the others. If there's no label, look for the one breaker that looks different from the rest. Flip the breaker back on, then test the lights and appliances in the relevant area one at a time.

CHAPTER

3

Clothing & Laundry

KEEP YOUR CLOTHES LOOKING BRAND NEW

Whether you can flawlessly fold a fitted sheet or you don't get why shirts come with extra buttons, there's always room to level up your laundry/clothing skills.

This chapter is all about how to care for your **clothing**, from the basics of **washing** and folding to some little tricks, quick fixes, and DIY tips. It's full of info to help you keep your favorite stuff in good shape—and make the whole process less of, well, a chore.

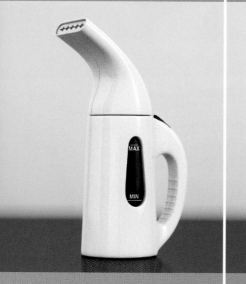

5 *Laundry Basics You Should Own*

If you're moving into a new place and need to buy all the household things, or if you've never regularly done your laundry before, here's what you need to get set up like a good laundry-doing adult. (There are plenty of additional products you can buy or make later; these are just the basics.)

1. Detergent for machine washing.

2. Gentle detergent for hand-washing.

3. A laundry hamper, basket, or bag—basically, a way to transport your dirty clothes from your room (or wherever) to your laundry room—whether that's in your house or in your building's basement.

4. A drying rack. This can be a super simple fold-up model.

5. An iron and ironing board if you wear any clothes that wrinkle. If you're really anti-ironing, at least get a small travel steamer in case of extreme rumpling.

Remove Pet Hair from Your Clothes

White fur all over your black outfit? As with upholstered furniture, you can clean fur from clothing with anything sticky. A lint roller is ideal, but tape will do the trick too—the thicker the better. Swiping over a surface with rubber gloves or dryer sheets can also take away some of that fluff.

And before you wash those clothes, give them a quick spin in the dryer. The hairs will get pulled into the lint trap.

Put a Sock in It

Keep socks (and gloves) together with their mates by employing a sock clip. Or get more bang for your buck with a mesh laundry bag, which not only keeps pairs together but also protects delicate items from rips and snags in the washer and dryer.

Zip It Up

The next time you encounter a frustratingly sticky zipper, try this trick: Rub wax paper along the teeth of the zipper to make pulling the tab easier. Don't have wax paper? Use a dry bar of soap! Bonus: Your hoodie will smell like a fresh breeze.

Get Rid of That Smell on New Jeans

New black or dark blue jeans can smell, uh, alarming. That's because formaldehyde used in the dying process stays in the denim. To get rid of the smell, first try hanging the offending denim in fresh air overnight. If that doesn't help, flip your jeans inside out and machine wash or soak in cold water and baking soda, borax, castile soap, or white vinegar. If you're still smelling the stench, use an oxygen bleach wash, following the directions on the package.

Wash Then Wear

New clothing is often treated with potentially irritating chemicals, including dyes and fabric softeners, and they've been touched by many hands. So always wash new clothes before wearing—that is *not* how you want your unboxing to go viral.

3 Ways to Whiten Whites

Keeping white clothes white is no easy job. Put on rubber gloves, and never mix bleach and ammonia!

1. Pour 16 cups water into a tub. Add ¼ cup bleach. Submerge items in the tub and let soak for 10 minutes. Then squeeze out clothing, rinse, and rewash. Repeat if needed.

2. Pour equal parts ammonia and liquid dish soap into a tub. Stir with an old toothbrush. Add clothing, then use the toothbrush to scrub. Soak for 30 minutes. Rinse clothing in water. Then wash and repeat if needed.

3. Add one part water and one part peroxide to a tub. Submerge garments and soak for 30 minutes. Rinse, rewash, and repeat if needed.

How Often to Wash Things

- **Bedding:** Aim to wash your bedsheets and pillowcases once a week. You may want to wash pillowcases more often if acne is a concern. Wash blankets, pillows, and duvet covers once a month, and comforters and bed skirts once or twice a year.
- **Towels:** Guidelines on how often to wash towels range from once a week to after every three or four uses to after every use. And if you can't do laundry that often, at least swap your used, damp, or smelly towels for fresh ones. When you do get to the laundry, wash towels separately on hot, and tumble dry.
- **Clothes:** Just as "one size fits all" clothes are a lie, there's no single answer to how often your garments need to be washed. It depends on the item, how long you wore it, how closely it fits

to the body, and whether It's likely to get dirty. Workout gear, underwear, and socks need to be washed after every wear. Shirts usually do too, though you might get two wears out of a shirt. Pants, skirts, and dresses can go several wears between washing or perhaps more, depending on the material, what activities you did, and whether you got sweaty doing them. Treat sweaters like shirts if you don't wear another shirt under them; if you layer, sweaters can be washed less frequently. Jeans are controversial—some swear they should almost never be washed! But do wash them if they're visibly dirty or smell bad. And remember that pajamas, loungewear, and bathrobes are also clothes, and thus need to be washed regularly too.

Read the Fine Print

Before you wash anything, especially if it's brand new, read the label. If you can't make heads or tails of those enigmatic laundry symbols (and who can?), print out an explainer and tape it to your washing machine.

Assemble a Simple Sewing Kit

Even if you prefer to go to a professional for alterations and major repairs, you can do a lot at home with the most basic sewing skills and an equally simple sewing kit. Here's what belongs in your DIY sewing starter kit:

- Needles (preferably a pack containing a few different sizes) and thread (preferably in a sampler with multiple colors).
- Safety pins. They often come in packs with several sizes, which is very useful.
- Double-sided fabric tape or hemming tape. When you don't have time or energy to sew, this is a great temporary alternative for sticking two pieces of fabric together.

- Straight pins (and a pin cushion).
- Small pair of sharp sewing scissors.
- A measuring tape. (The soft kind.)
- Optional: a seam ripper, thimble, and, if you have trouble with that crucial first step, a needle threader.

4 Sneaky Clothing Fix Hacks

To look way more together than you are, keep these little secrets in your closet in case of tiny clothing catastrophes:

1. Hem tape: No sewing required with this transparent, double-sided, and surprisingly tough tape. It can even see your hastily hemmed garment through several machine washes!

2. Bra clips: When you need a racer-back bra, like, yesterday, these little clips can come to your rescue. They can also keep straps hidden under your boatneck when you need to look all refined.

3. Clear nail polish and surgical tape: Both can save nickel-allergic peeps from the annoying rash from that annoyingly placed metal button.

4. Hair elastics: If your zipper is slipping down, use a small hair elastic to attach the zipper's pull tab to the button of your pants. You can also use an elastic band to give yourself a few inches of breathing room in tight trousers, as long as your waistband is covered by your shirt.

Restring a Drawstring

If your drawstring disappears into one side of your waistband or hood, you can pull it out and rethread it with a safety pin. Attach the pin to one end of the string, then slide it through the eyelet on one side. Push the pin, bunching up the fabric around it, then pull, straightening the fabric as the pin advances. (Think inchworm.) Repeat until the pin emerges from the other side.

Fix a Ripped Seam

Being ripped apart at the seams sounds dramatic, but if you're a shirt, it's no big deal. It's also very easy to repair! So get a needle, some thread (preferably matching the thread that's there already), and, optional but helpful, a few straight pins and a pair of scissors. First, flip the garment inside out. Then pin the two sides together so they lie flat. Sew along the rip until it is closed. Sew back over the raw edges of the rip—meaning, the edge of the fabric itself. Tie off and cut the thread.

Fix a Snagged Thread

If a thread gets snagged out of place in your knit top or sweater, don't worry—but don't just leave it or cut it and assume everything will be fine. (Both nonsolutions can lead to a larger hole.) Instead, use the blunt end of a sewing needle to carefully nudge the thread back through to the inside until it falls back into place. If it's easier, you can use the needle's pointy end to gently grab the misbehaving thread from the inside and pull it back through. Once the outside of the garment is smooth, make a small knot on the inside so the thread doesn't slip out again.

Understanding Soap Nuts

First of all...soap nuts aren't nuts. They're dried berries (no nut allergy worries here!) from the *Sapindus mukorossi* tree, and they double as an all-natural soap. To use them, just toss them in the washer instead of detergent. These gentle, reusable, compostable little laundry helpers are also eco-friendly; they produce less waste than traditional detergents and can be grown without pesticides.

5 Earth-Friendly Laundry Options

If you're making small changes to your routines to be a little more eco-conscious, try these laundry room swaps:

1. **Trade your regular detergent for an eco-friendly one.** These are made without certain harmful ingredients and are often refillable, eliminating excess packaging and reducing plastic waste.

2. **Choose eco-smart pods.** Look for biodegradable detergent pods, which dole out single servings of environmentally friendly detergent in packaging that won't hang around forever.

3. **Try laundry tablets.** These have even less packaging and, when combined with water, make an easy-to-use and eco-friendly laundry soap.

4. **Skip fabric softener and use wool dryer balls instead.** They soften the same while shortening drying time and being all-natural and reusable.

5. **Don't run the dryer when you don't have to.** When possible, air-dry instead.

Ditch the Plastic Laundry Hamper

Here are some hamper options that double as decor:

- **Linen-lined baskets:** They can have a metal, wire, or wood frame, but they all turn into an easy-to-carry bag.
- **Vintage laundry bags:** These are a charming choice.
- **Rolling bins:** If stairs aren't involved, a retro wheeled hamper, usually lined with cloth, is cute and convenient.

Let Baking Soda Save the Day

What *can't* this stuff do? It makes your baked goods fluffy, it cleans your house, and it helps you do laundry.

- To pretreat stinky, sweaty shirts, add water to baking soda until you have a paste. Apply and scrub it into the affected areas with an old toothbrush, then let sit several hours before washing.
- To get clothes cleaner and whites whiter, just add ½ cup of baking soda to your regular wash.

Use Vinegar and Hydrogen Peroxide

White vinegar and hydrogen peroxide (the 3% kind sold in drugstores) can work wonders in your washing machine:

- Vinegar: Wash each load once with 2 cups white vinegar, then again with detergent.
- Hydrogen peroxide: Use it in your washer to whiten whites (add 1 cup before you put in laundry) or brighten brights (add 1 cup hydrogen peroxide plus 2 cups water before putting in your clothes).

5 Ways to Do Less Laundry

The easiest and fastest way to do laundry...is to *not* do it at all. Here's how:

1. Make an effort to avoid getting clothes dirty or crumpled when possible. Change out of nice outfits before doing messy tasks, and put clothes away when you're not wearing them.

2. Try to catch and treat stains quickly; for minor spills, you might not need to wash the item if it's otherwise clean.

3. Remember that aside from shirts, socks, exercise wear, and underwear, most pieces of clothing don't need to be washed after every wear.

4. To go longer between each wash, stock up on essentials that do need to be laundered frequently.

5. If you don't mind the chore per se but want to cut down on trips to the laundromat or energy consumption, wash clothes by hand and air-dry whenever you can.

Remove Paint from Clothes

Got dried paint on your clothes? Get it off with rubbing alcohol. Just scrub some on with a toothbrush, then wipe the fabric with a sponge. This trick also works on shoes and carpets. (As with any treatment, when in doubt, do a patch test first in a hidden area of the item to be sure it's safe for that type of fabric.)

Pamper Your Delicates

Delicates are, basically, items of clothing that are easy to ruin. Think about silks and their synthetic cousins, lace tops, high-quality knitwear, or anything beaded or shaped with wires. Here's how to care for them without destroying them:

- Treat stains while they're still wet. But don't just dump any cleanser on your bougie blouse: Take a minute to look up the best cleaning method for the fabric and the particular stain.
- Wash delicates separately in the washing machine on a gentle cycle.
- If the label doesn't provide specific washing directions, use cold water, gentle detergent, and the delicate or short cycle—or wash by hand.
- Dry flat unless the label instructs otherwise.
- Wash in a mesh bag to prevent snags.
- Steam, don't iron. But if you must iron, turn the garment inside out and put the iron on the lowest setting. Then place a tea towel or pillowcase over the item before ironing.

Stop Clothes from Fading

Here's a super easy way to keep dark and brightly colored clothes from fading: Wash them inside out. Bonus: It also helps fragile embellishments and buttons stay attached longer.

Make Reusable Lavender Fabric Softener Sponges

You don't need to buy fabric softener sheets!

YOU DO NEED:

- **Baking soda**
- **A glass container with a lid**
- **Hot water**
- **White vinegar**
- **Lavender essential oil**
- **Kitchen sponges**

HERE'S WHAT TO DO:

1. Pour ½ cup baking soda into the container.

2. Add 1 cup hot water into the baking soda and stir gently.

3. Slowly pour ½ cup vinegar into the mixture and stir.

4. Add 10 drops lavender essential oil to the container.

5. Place sponges in the container and seal shut.

   To use a fabric softener sponge, give the container a good shake to mix the solution around. Select a sponge and squeeze out the excess fluid. Add it to your laundry when you place it in the dryer. Once the laundry is finished, place the sponge back in the container for future use.

Throw a Tennis Ball in Your Dryer

When you're drying something with stuffing—think puffer jacket, comforter, or pillow—throw a tennis ball in the dryer too. (Use a clean new one, not one the dog has been chewing.) The bouncing ball will help keep your stuff fluffed up and prevent it from getting weirdly lumpy.

Clean Your Dryer's Lint Trap

Yep, you need to worry about dryer lint traps in adulthood. Here's a good habit to get into: Every time you do laundry, take half a second to clean out your dryer's lint trap. If you let too much of that fluff back up in there, it can turn into a dangerous fire.

Air Your ~~Dirty~~ Clean Laundry

In this case, air-*dry* your clean laundry! You can air-dry everything if you want to, but you should always air-dry clothes with rubber, elastic, or wire in them (e.g., sweatpants, bras); delicate items (e.g., lacy or sequined tops); sweaters; and anything that tells you not to put it in the dryer on the tag.

Avoid Static Cling

No one wants their clothes sticking to them like glue. Grab a dryer sheet and rub it over your clinging clothes. Even better, get a can of antistatic spray to have on hand for future clinginess.

Dry Your Clothes Faster

Want your clothes to dry a little faster? Put a clean, dry towel in the dryer with damp items to speed up drying time.

Sew on a
BUTTON

Buttons are always finding ways to get loose or fall off entirely, so you might as well learn to fix them yourself. Luckily, all you need is the original button (or a replacement), a needle, and thread.

WHAT YOU NEED:

- Thread in the same color as the button
- Needle
- Scissors

HOW TO DO IT:

1. Thread your needle, making a knot near the end of the thread.

2. Line up your button and poke the needle from the inside of the garment out through one of the holes in the button.

3. Now sew in and out of all four holes in the button, making an X shape with your thread until the button feels tightly attached.

4. Finally, wrap the thread around the base of the button, then tie off and cut your thread.

Stash Away Those Extra Buttons!

Every time you get a new piece of clothing that comes with a little baggie or envelope of extra buttons and thread samples, squirrel them away for the future. Even if you never need to make a repair on that particular garment, your stash of extras could come in handy another time. (Store them all together, in a dedicated jar or tin, so you won't have to rummage around looking when that time comes.)

Don't Get Taken to the Cleaners

Dry cleaning is expensive, and the chemicals used in the process can be harmful to the environment. To cut down on dry cleaning, take good care of your clothes and spot-treat stains yourself when you can. Also, when buying new clothes, look for items that don't require dry cleaning.

And know that sometimes "dry-clean only" isn't a *strict* rule. Take structured pieces, severe stains, and tricky materials to the pros, but if you're willing, wash wool and silk items carefully by hand.

Check Your Pockets

Before you put that pair of jeans or shirt or hoodie in the washing machine, check its pockets. You don't need to literally launder money, and you *really* don't want to wash and dry tissues.

Place a small trash bin and a little coin dish in your laundry area so you don't just transfer this stuff to the pockets of what you're currently wearing, creating an endless cycle of potential laundry mishaps.

Measure Your Detergent

Sometimes, more isn't better—it can be worse! Think salt on your food or product in your hair. In this vein, pouring more laundry soap into the washer won't get your clothes cleaner. In fact, too much detergent can leave your garments covered in a residue that stiffens the fabric. Besides, pouring too much soap in the washer is a total waste of money. Check the package directions and only use what you really need.

Lighten the (Laundry) Load

It may seem like you're saving time, but don't try to stuff as much laundry as you possibly can into a single load. It might fit, but it can cause the washer to overheat and/or not clean clothes very well. Plus, even if they survive the washing part unscathed, that many clothes will probably dry unevenly at best.

Separate Your Laundry

Separating laundry is simple: Just don't put the red sweatshirt in with the white sheets unless you want them to be pink, right? Well, yes...but there's a little more to it than that.

First, you should be washing dark, light, and white clothes separately. You should also be doing separate loads for towels, sheets, and delicates. This lets you use the proper setting for each type of load and protects more fragile items from getting pushed around and damaged by tougher ones.

Make it easier for yourself by sorting at the laundry hamper stage and not the "It's midnight and I have nothing to wear tomorrow" stage.

Make Your Own Natural Laundry Detergent

If store-bought detergent is too expensive or feels harsh on your skin, you can make an easy all-natural alternative using castile soap. Just add 1 cup of it to 2¼ cups of water, along with ¾ cup of baking soda and ¼ cup of salt. To wash, use ¼ cup of this mix per load.

Hang Up a Long Dress in a Short Closet

If you like maxis and your closet is built for minis, try these creative folding methods and stop sweeping your closet floor with your hems:

- **Option 1:** Lay the dress flat on your bed and fold it in thirds lengthwise. Then fold the skirt, at about a foot from the bottom of the dress, over the flat bar of the hanger. Pull the hanger up, then slip the dress's straps over the top part of the hanger.

- **Option 2:** Start folding as in Option 1, but after pulling the hanger up, hang the top of the dress on a second hanger. Then either hang the bottom hanger over the neck of the top one or hang them side by side in your closet.

Sell, Donate, or Recycle Unwanted Clothes

You just decluttered your closet. Partying face emoji! Now you have to decide what to do with the clothes you don't want. Loudly crying face emoji! Here's how to split that pile of nos into piles of sell, donate, or recycle:

- Consider **selling** clothing that's in very good condition (especially if it's unworn or like new). Special vintage pieces and new, in season, trending pieces are easier to sell than anything in the middle.

- **Donate** clothes that are in good, wearable condition, but aren't particularly valuable for resale. Or donate all clothes in good shape to avoid the hassle of selling.

- Find **textile recycling** for clothes that are stained, damaged, or otherwise unwearable. Or consider turning these clothes into cleaning rags or find other purposes for them.

Fold a Fitted Sheet

Does anyone really know how to fold a fitted sheet? For real though, here's how:

1. Lay the sheet out with the elasticated part facing up.

2. Stick your hand into one corner pocket, then place that covered hand inside the corner pocket that would go on the same side of the bed if the fitted sheet was, well, fitted.

3. Do the same on the other side, so the other two corners are nestled one inside the other.

4. Smooth the sheet out while retaining the tucks you just made. You'll have a square with a small elastic circle in its center. Fold the bottom third of that square up toward the center, and the top third down over it. You'll now have a narrow rectangle with the elastic parts concealed.

5. Smooth with your hands, then fold both ends of the rectangle in toward the center.

6. Finally, tuck one end into the other, creating a smooth bundle that won't come unfurled.

Upcycle Damaged Clothing

If you can't fix a damaged clothing item but you still love it, go with the situation and mess the piece up further until it's fashion. Torn jacket? Iron on some patches that make a statement. Paint splatter on your pants? Add more to make it look intentional. Jeans worn in a weird spot? Distress that denim with sandpaper. Rip or stain near the top, bottom, or sleeve of a T-shirt? Grab some scissors and make a custom scoop neck or sleeveless cropped top.

6 Ironing Basics to Know

These days, some people pride themselves on never ironing anything. Don't tell them, but they sometimes look like the airline lost their luggage and they've been wearing that outfit for a week. If you don't want to look like that, learn these simple ironing rules:

1. Different fabrics require different iron settings—basically, more or less heat. Always make sure you're using the correct setting for the fabric you're ironing. Delicate and synthetic fabrics need very little heat, while thicker, natural fibers need more. There should be a little guide, with numbers, printed right on your iron; when in doubt, start cooler.

2. When ironing multiple items, start with the lightest clothing that needs the coolest setting first, then work up, ironing the heaviest items that require the highest heat last.

3. Use the steam setting for garments that are very wrinkled or directly on creases.

4. If you're ironing structured or pleated items—think pleats and shirt collars—try spray starch to keep them looking sharp.

5. When ironing collars and cuffs, smooth out wrinkles on the inside, then finish up by pressing the outside.

6. Iron carefully around embellishments, zippers, buttons, etc. to avoid creating a weird puckering effect.

5 Ironing Don'ts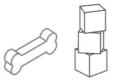

Ironing is one of those chores where the consequences of messing up can range from being annoyed to being hospitalized. Neither of those are much fun, so iron carefully.

1. Never leave an iron that's turned on unattended—it can easily tip, fall, or burn a hole in something. If you have children or pets, don't leave an iron alone even if it's off (they take awhile to cool down completely and are heavy!), especially if it's still plugged in.

2. Don't iron anything that's stained or smells bad. It will only get worse, and harder to remove, if it's set in place with added heat.

3. Don't try to multitask while you iron. Like curling wands or frying pans, irons can go from helpful tools to instruments of burning pain in an instant.

4. Don't damage delicates; always iron flimsier fabrics inside out. (For added protection, place a pillowcase or other piece of clean cloth over lightweight clothing when ironing.)

5. Don't drip. If you're using the steam setting, make sure the iron is fully warmed up before you start. This will stop the water from dripping onto your clothes.

No Iron? No Steamer? No Problem.

When you're stuck without an iron but you don't want to look like you slept in those clothes, try these hacks:

- If you have time, put the item on a hanger (gravity alone will help) and hang it in the bathroom while you shower (steam will help more).
- Add a tablespoon of fabric softener to 8 ounces of water. Using a spray bottle, apply to the crinkled clothing and lay flat or hang up until dry.
- If you don't have much time, repurpose a hair straightener as an iron and (carefully) smooth crumpled clothes.
- Spritz clothing with water from a spray bottle and aim your hair dryer at the wrinkles to release them.

Don't Leave Clothes in the Washer or Dryer Too Long

A couple hours is no big deal. But if you leave wet clothes in the washer overnight or longer, they can start to smell funky and will need to be washed again. In the dryer, they can get wrinkly if ignored too long. If another spin around doesn't sort them, you'll probably need to iron them.

Brighten Up Your Laundry Room

Laundry rooms can look pretty blah, especially if they're not rooms but weird little afterthought areas. But you can brighten yours up and make doing laundry seem a lot more appealing.

- Install a floating shelf above the washer and dryer for easy access to detergents and other necessities.
- Mount a drying rack to the wall that pulls out or flips down, Murphy bed–style, when you need it.
- Use matching storage boxes to hold soaps and other things on open shelves. This simple adjustment can instantly take an area from utilitarian to charming.
- If your laundry area is in a hall or part of another room, and you want to hide it but can't add a door, hang a curtain to conceal it. Use a tension rod or traditional wall-mounted rod depending on the configuration of the space. Pick an attractive curtain that blends in with the area.

Clean Your Laundry Area

Think how jealous your washer and dryer will get if they always see you cleaning clothes, but you never clean *them*.

To clean a washing machine, run it on hot with 2 cups of hydrogen peroxide or (not and!) 1 cup of white vinegar.

Clean the exterior of the washer and dryer as you'd wipe any surface.

If you have a separate laundry room, don't forget to wash the floor and keep surfaces wiped and dusted.

And while you're at it, clean your (cool, unplugged) iron every so often. Using a paste of baking soda and water, lightly scrub then wipe with a cloth dampened in white vinegar. Clean your ironing board cover too; just throw it in the washer.

Clean Your Baseball Hat... in the Dishwasher?

That's right! Place the hat on the top rack and use dish detergent and a low heat setting. If you want to, you can even buy a hat form, which helps your cap keep its shape in the washer. Just please don't wash headwear with tableware.

BTW, if you have a vintage baseball cap, it probably has a cardboard brim; these can only be spot-cleaned. Just scrub with a toothbrush dipped in a water and laundry detergent solution.

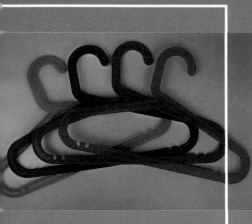

5 Clothes Closet Mistakes to Avoid

If you want to preserve and protect your wardrobe, here's what *not* to do:

1. Don't leave dry cleaning bags on. Far from protecting clothes, the chemicals in the bag can actually mess up fabrics long term, so remove them when you get home.

2. Don't use cheap wire hangers. They can cause discoloration, creases, or tears. Get the best hangers you can (which don't have to be fancy but should at least be smooth).

3. Don't leave buttons and zippers undone. Close up your clothing so it won't slouch itself out of shape.

4. Don't hang or fold messily, cramming items into a too-small space. This can lead to creases, pulls, snags, and general wear and tear. Give clothes the space they need.

5. Don't put dirty or smelly clothes back in the closet. Stains get harder to clean the longer they set, and organic matter (like sweat) can attract critters.

Take Care of Your Sweaters

Sweater weather isn't all leaves and lattes. Here's how to keep your coziest clothes looking their best:

• Don't hang sweaters in the closet; keep them folded to avoid stretching their fibers over time.
  If you have to hang, fold the sweater over the hanger like a pair of trousers.
• Wash sweaters on the correct setting (or by hand) and lay flat to dry unless the label specifies otherwise.
• Remove pills using a battery-operated fabric shaver, sweater comb, disposable razor,
  sewing scissors, or a pumice stone.

Keep Your Sneakers Clean

We can debate whether they're sneakers, tennis shoes, trainers, gym shoes, kicks, or whatever new word the kids invented yesterday, but everyone would agree they shouldn't be caked in mud. Here's how to clean them up.

First, remove any dirt that you can brush away. Remove the laces and insoles, if possible, and clean them with a baking soda and water paste. Many sneakers, both leather and fabric, can be cleaned in the washing machine. (Check the label first.) Wash in a mesh bag, in warm water on a regular cycle, and add some towels to balance the load. Or clean sneakers by hand with a toothbrush or other soft brush and a gentle liquid laundry detergent. (Use a Magic Eraser to clean scuffs from white sneakers.) Let them air-dry.

Unshrink Shrunken Clothes

No, you didn't get bigger overnight; you shrank your clothes. Here's how to try to get them back to their original size.

Add 1 tablespoon of hair conditioner to 1 liter of warm water in a bowl. Put the shrunken item in and soak it for 30 minutes. Then lightly squeeze to remove excess water and lay the clothing out flat on a dry towel. Carefully roll it up to absorb the liquid. Then stretch the garment out over a second dry towel and clip it to the edges of the towels with clothespins. Let it air-dry.

Make Your Own Pretreater Spray

Try making this homemade pretreater so you can address stains ASAP: Mix one part dish soap and two parts hydrogen peroxide, then pour into a small spray bottle. When a stain strikes, blot the affected area with a damp paper towel, then spray on your magic mixture. Wait 10 minutes, then blot. Let dry for 20 minutes. Then wash as usual.

Treat Stains on the Go

If you're prone to spilling food on yourself, raise your hand! (You knocked over a coffee cup while doing that, didn't you?) Reverse the damage anywhere by keeping some store-bought detergent wipes or pens in your bag, desk, or car.

Get Makeup Stains Out of Clothes

It's supposed to go on your face, but it often ends up on your shirt. Here's how to pretend that never happened:

- Remove **foundation stains** with liquid detergent—pour directly on the stain, scrub, then machine wash on the hottest setting appropriate for the garment. You can also try shaving cream or shampoo.
- Clean up a **lipstick stain** with dish soap, hair spray, rubbing alcohol, or, in a pinch, makeup remover cloths.
- For **eye shadow or mascara**, use makeup remover just as you would on your face.

Get Gum Out of Clothes

There's nothing worse than realizing you've been sitting on gum. Here's what to do: Put the pants in a plastic bag in the freezer for several hours. Then use a butter knife to scrape the sticky goo off.

9 Weird Stain Hacks

Usually, the solution to stained clothes is laundry detergent (or baking soda). But sometimes, the answer is lurking where you least expect it. File these little tricks away for your next mishap:

1. Help **tomato-based stains** fade with the power of the sun: Just hang the garment in the sunlight while it's still wet.

2. Get rid of a **chocolate stain** with toothpaste. Dampen fabric, apply a dab of toothpaste, and rub; add a little baking soda if it needs some help.

3. Tackle an **ink stain** with hand sanitizer or hair spray. Just cover the stain, let it sit for 10 minutes, and wash.

4. Rub chalk into **grease stains** to absorb the oil. Baby powder works too!

5. Dab rubbing alcohol on an **acrylic paint stain**. Then rub the stain away.

6. If a **blood** stain is dry, wet with cold water. Apply pretreater, followed by a water and ammonia solution. Then wash with cold water using enzyme-based detergent.

7. Rub **sweat** with bar soap before washing. If fabric is discolored, soak the garment in white vinegar and hot water. Wash normally.

8. Blot up a **red wine** stain, adding water if it's dried. Apply salt to absorb liquid. Rinse in hot water before washing normally. Still stained? Use hot water and white vinegar or oxygen-based detergent.

9. Apply pretreater to **grass stains** and let sit for 15 minutes. Then scrub from the center of the stain outward. Wash with enzyme-based detergent.

4

Cooking & Entertaining

PREPARE AND PRESENT FOOD LIKE A PRO

Preparing and eating food have been essential parts of human life since the first humans sat down for a meal of woolly mammoth. So why does every step of the process seem so difficult?

That's why this chapter is focused on going back to basics. You'll find entry-level **cooking** lessons, food tips and tricks, and some **hosting** and dining rules you might have forgotten—or never picked up—along the way. Plus, you'll be inspired to get creative and actually enjoy the experience!

20 Kitchen Tools You Need

It's always a good idea to set yourself up with a decent set of tools and utensils:

- At least one of the following: pots, frying pans, baking trays, baking tins
- Pot holders
- Tongs
- A set of measuring cups and spoons
- A grater
- A vegetable peeler
- A can opener
- A whisk
- A slotted spoon

- A ladle
- A spatula
- A funnel
- A colander
- A strainer
- Kitchen scissors
- A wooden spoon
- A timer
- A cutting board
- A few decent knives
- A set of mixing bowls

Baking vs. Cooking

These are technically two different things! Cooking, generally speaking, means preparing, mixing, and heating foods to make them edible and tasty. Baking is a form of cooking that does this using dry heat within an enclosed space. Colloquially, though, when people talk about baking vs. cooking, baking refers to making "baked goods" like breads, cakes, cookies, pies, and the like, while cooking refers to preparing basically every other kind of dish. Including, well, baked potatoes.

How to Read a Recipe

If you find the language of recipes off-putting, don't be intimidated. Here are some tips for reading any recipe:

- Start with recipes accompanied by photos. Your finished product doesn't have to look perfect, but pics are a helpful guide for colors, textures, and plating.
- Read the recipe thoroughly first. This will tell you if it requires any special ingredients or equipment and how much time you'll need to cook the dish.
- If you encounter a term you've never heard before, look it up. It's probably nothing too difficult, just French.
- Don't avoid recipes just because they use unfamiliar measurements. You can convert grams to ounces or milliliters to cups with a few clicks.
- Everyone LOLs at the essays that preface recipes on food blogs, and they can be pretty cringe. But do skim that text; it might contain a helpful tip.

Preheating Does Matter

Most recipes call for preheating the oven, and it can feel like an extra step put there just to make your life harder. So does it really matter? Well, yes. Because while you might be able to get away without doing it on occasion, failing to preheat can cause a recipe to turn out badly or simply not cook fully—ironically meaning your rush to get that food in the oven quicker will ultimately make the cooking time longer.

Clean As You Go

The last thing you want to do after enjoying a meal you've spent an hour preparing is to clean up a kitchen that looks like a tornado hit it. To avoid this fate, clean up as you cook. While you're waiting for that onion to soften in the pan, see if anything can go in the dishwasher or back in the cabinet.

5 Ways to Make Food Last Longer

Storing your food right will help keep it edible longer, which means less food wasted in the trash or compost and less money wasted in the store. Win-win!

1. Place a couple apples in with your potatoes to prevent sprouting.

2. Add a few grains of rice to your salt or sugar shaker to absorb moisture. No more clumps!

3. Keep lettuce longer by wrapping it in a paper towel and placing it in a plastic bag in the fridge.

4. Preserve onions in the legs of a pair of stockings, tying knots in between.

5. Freeze flour in an airtight container. Just bring it to room temp before baking.

Eat on the Go

Eating on the go may not be glam, but it can be healthy and convenient. Here are some tips:

1. Fruit fits in your hand and comes with its own wrapper: There's a reason it's sometimes called the original fast food.

2. Trail mix is light, portable, and hearty enough to keep you going all day. Make your own with dried fruit, nuts, seeds, chocolate chips, coconut flakes, mini-pretzels, or anything you like.

3. Snacks with sauces aren't off-limits. Just pop a small plastic cup (e.g., from single-serve packs of applesauce) in the mouth of a Mason jar, and another between the lid and the seal. Then transport your yogurt, berries, and granola—or salad, croutons, and dressing—together, yet separately.

Shop Smart

First, never shop for food while hungry. Those brightly colored, expensive bags of snacks look even more tempting when you're ravenous. Second, maintain a running shopping list—on paper or on your phone—to have at the ready when you shop.

4 Batch Cooking Tips

Meal prepping and batch cooking is a popular way to avoid cooking every day. Here's how to make it go smoothly:

1. Block off a chunk of the day (say, a weekend morning) to cook for the week ahead.

2. Make sure you have pots and pans large enough to make all this food.

3. Choose and label your containers wisely. Ideally, you want to store your portions in containers that can handle hot and frozen food and potentially be portable (if you're taking it to work or school).

4. Give yourself options by prepping the base of your meal but leaving toppings off so you can add some variety.

Try Ingredient Prepping

If the concept of meal prepping makes you tired, try just preparing ingredients instead. Here are some examples:

- Place washed, sliced vegetables and fruits in airtight containers for instant snacks and cooking ingredients.
- Portion out protein and freeze (write the contents and date on the freezer bag), so when you want two servings of chicken, you won't have to deal with a full 1½ pounds of the stuff.
- Cook rice, pasta, and potatoes ahead of time to make a base for meals for the next couple days.
- Freeze bananas that you can't eat in time for later use in smoothies.
- When you make sauces, cook more than you need and freeze for use in the future.

Personalize the Party

Having people over? Make your guests feel special (and prevent drink mix-ups) by adding individual touches to glasses and place settings. Wine glass charms for stemmed glasses come in every imaginable variety, or you can make your own with supplies from the craft store. For stemless glasses, look for charms that stick magnetically to the side or clip on the rim. (Who doesn't love a little umbrella?)

Place cards are also easy to make and to personalize, or you can write guests' names on their glasses (and plates) with food-safe markers.

Throw a Summer Celebration

Cool down with ice cream cake pops. Crumble yellow cake into a bowl. Stir in ½ cup of vanilla frosting. Spoon dollops of the mixture into an ice cube tray. Divide 1 cup of softened vanilla ice cream, 1 cup of crushed cookies, and 1 cup of softened chocolate ice cream among the cubes. Freeze for 30 minutes. Place a stick in the center of each cube and freeze until solid. Melt 2 cups of white chocolate and dip each cube into it.

Host a Fall Fete

For sweater weather vibes, make grown-up versions of fall childhood faves. For example, try these easy (and less messy) caramel apples: Cut apples in half lengthwise, scooping out the core. Then pop two small caramel candies inside. Wrap the apples in aluminum foil, then bake for 30 minutes on the flames of your firepit (or in your oven).

Welcome Winter with a Party

When it's cold outside, invite friends over to warm up at a cozy get-together. One option: Set out a hot cocoa bar with different types of cocoa and milk and a range of marshmallows from mini to extra large. Provide a few flavorings, like cinnamon sticks and mint syrup, and toppings, like whipped cream, drizzly chocolate, and caramel sauce.

Plan a Spring Gathering

Celebrate the coming of spring with these colorful cupcakes: Mix cake frosting in six small bowls with a drop of food coloring gel in red, orange, yellow, green, blue, and purple. Use piping bags to draw a stripe of each color on a sheet of plastic wrap. Then roll the plastic wrap into a cylinder and insert it in a fresh piping bag to ice cupcakes.

Host a Top-Notch Potluck

Hosting a BYO-style meal? Here's how to make sure it goes smoothly (and you don't end up with ten bowls of dip and no chips):

- If it makes the planning easier for you, pick a food theme and let everyone know it. If this seems like an unnecessary restriction, then don't!
- Assign or let guests choose general food categories (mains, sides, desserts, etc.). Don't micromanage, but do let your baking-obsessed friend bring the cake while suggesting something that isn't cake to the friend who asks, "What should I bring?"
- If you're not providing drinks, plates, napkins, cups, and utensils, make sure someone else is.
- For larger gatherings (or if your group is really organized), consider a virtual sign-up sheet.
- Have serving spoons and basic condiments, like salt and pepper, on hand in case guests (understandably) forget to bring these.

Eat Your Veggies

Ah, vegetables. If you didn't like them as a kid and never learned to as an adult, there's a good chance you've just never tried them cooked the right way for you. It's easy to boil broccoli into a bland mush or toughen it up by baking it too long. Many people have been surprised to happen upon the right recipe and belatedly discover a love for Brussels sprouts or kale.

Also, lots of vegetables can taste totally different when eaten cooked vs. raw. So even if you hate carrot sticks, roasted carrots could still be your new favorite thing.

And aside from different cooking techniques and seasonings, there's a mind-blowing variety of vegetables out there. If you grew up thinking lettuce, cucumbers, and tomatoes (technically a fruit, but they've earned their place in the salad) were the whole story, seek out some Swiss chard or spaghetti squash and do a taste test.

Ripen Unripe Fruit

When the fruit isn't ready, but you are:

1. Place bananas in a rolled-up paper bag with a tomato or an apple. Leave the bag on the counter overnight.

2. Wrap an avocado in aluminum foil. Place it on a baking sheet and bake at 200°F for 10 minutes.

3. Place a mango in a plastic container and cover it with uncooked rice. Put the lid on the container and let it sit for 1–3 days.

4. Chop the top off a pineapple, then place it cut side down on a plate and cover with plastic wrap. Leave it in the fridge for 2 days.

5. Place stone fruits stem down on a linen or cotton cloth. Cover with another cloth. Let sit for 1–2 days.

Don't Wash That Fruit (Yet)

It's obviously very important to wash produce before you eat it (you do not want to eat soil, pesticide residue, and bacteria). But don't wash your fruit the minute you bring it home and pop it in the fridge. Washing right before eating instead will help the fruit last longer.

The exception to this rule: if you're prepping a bowl of cut fruit to have on hand as a fresh, grabbable snack. In that case, wash, chop, cover, refrigerate, and eat within a few days.

5 Impressive Little Food Hacks

When you pull out these unexpected fixes, you'll look like you know all the tricks:

1. Peel a mango with a drinking glass. Cut fruit into chunks lengthwise, then slide along the side of the glass, fruit inside and peel outside. Or score an X at the top and peel it like a banana.

2. Resuscitate hardened cookies by adding a slice of bread to their container overnight.

3. Soften stale bread by placing the loaf in a baking pan and pouring water on it. Then bake at 325°F for 8 minutes.

4. Peel fresh ginger with a plain old spoon.

5. Cut an onion without crying by chopping underwater. Or chill the onion in the fridge or freezer before cutting.

How to Bake a Potato

First, scrub the tater clean with water and a brush, and pat dry. Cut away any bad parts and stab a few times with your knife to let steam escape while cooking, preventing a potato-splosion. Place the potato on a baking sheet lined with aluminum foil and bake at around 400°F or 425°F for about an hour, adjusting time for the potato's size.

How to Separate an Egg

If you're new to cooking and baking, this might be a skill you don't have yet. Luckily, it's quite simple to separate eggs into their component parts. Carefully tap the eggshell against the edge of your bowl so a crack appears but the egg doesn't break. Then use your fingers to pry half of the shell up and open the egg, while holding it upright over a small bowl. Pull off the top half of the shell, letting most of the white spill into the bowl. Then transfer the yolk back and forth from one half of the shell to the other, holding one half shell in each hand, and let the rest of the white drip into the bowl. Then drop the yolk into a second small bowl.

How to Boil an Egg

It's actually pretty hard to ruin an egg in a pot of water. Simply place your eggs in a single layer in a pot. Don't crowd them. Cover them with cold water, then bring to a boil. Leave them boiling or remove from heat and cover. With either method, how long you leave them in hot water depends on how soft or hard you want your eggs; start with about 3 minutes for very soft eggs and go up to about 10 minutes for hard eggs. When they're done, run them under very cold water or place them in an ice bath.

Peel Garlic the Easy Way

Garlic, the allium with more packaging than a small item shipped in an extra-large box. Here's a quick technique to unwrap this flavorful little gift. Smash a head of garlic on the counter with the flat of your hand. Put the whole mess in a small bowl. Take a second bowl of the same size, flip it upside down, and place it on top of the first bowl. Shake vigorously (good opportunity for a 5-second kitchen dance here), and the garlic skin should come right off.

How to Pit an Avocado

Cut the avocado in half vertically along one side, and then the opposite side. Repeat to cut it into quarters. Gently pull each quarter apart away from the pit. Now peel each section and get that avo on your toast ASAP.

Learn Your Salts 101

So many salts, so little time. Here's what the most common types of salt are for:

- **Table salt** (or iodized salt) is dependable for salting pasta water or seasoning food before cooking and baking.
- **Kosher salt**, coarser than table salt, can be used for almost any purpose. (And all pure salt is naturally kosher; the kind sold as "kosher salt" is simply what's used in the process of making meat kosher.)
- **Sea salt** comes in different textures and colors and goes by different names depending on where in the world it's harvested. Sea salt is usually coarser, its taste is often more complex, and it's not fortified like table salt. In general, it's fancier and more costly, so think of sea salt as a special garnish and table salt as an everyday seasoning.
- Other types, like **pink Himalayan salt** and **Celtic Sea Salt**, periodically trend for their unusual look or purported health benefits and can be interesting to try, but they aren't a pantry must-have.
- **Black salt** has an egg-like flavor and is sometimes used to make vegan or otherwise egg-free dishes taste eggy.

5 Edible Party Favors

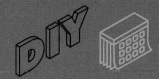

Want to send your guests home with a tasty little memento of the party? Make these cute favors, which are endlessly customizable for any occasion. (They're also good gifts to bring along to parties you attend!)

1. Spread microwave popcorn on parchment on a baking sheet. Drizzle melted white chocolate over popcorn. Add broken pretzel pieces and chocolate candies or chips. Add sprinkles. Scoop the cooled mixture into clear gift bags, tie with a ribbon, and attach a gift tag.

2. Fill a pretty glass jar with small candies. Close it up and tie a gift tag around the lid.

3. Place small foil-wrapped chocolates inside the wires of a whisk. Secure with cellophane wrapping. Use a nice ribbon to tie a gift tag around the handle.

4. Make a fancy variation on peanut butter. Mix peanut butter, melted white chocolate, and crushed chocolate cookies. Pour or scoop into a small glass jar. Affix a gift tag to the lid.

5. Fill three small glass containers with dehydrated milk, hot cocoa mix, and mini-marshmallows. Use tape to stack the containers vertically and decorate with a tag and ribbon.

Customize your favors by using specific holiday candies (e.g., candy corn for Thanksgiving) or colors symbolic of a holiday (e.g., red and green sprinkles and ribbons for Christmas). Add more unique touches by decorating containers using a hot glue gun and buttons, ribbons, felt, pipe cleaners, or any craft materials you choose.

Arrange a Charcuterie Board

They show no sign of going away, so you might as well learn how to make a scrumptious board.

1. Add a hard cheese, a slightly softer cubed cheese, a crumbly cheese, and a very soft cheese.

2. Fold cured meats into fan shapes.

3. Set out honey, mustard, pickles, nuts, and/or fruit preserves in small bowls.

4. Add fresh fruit, like a bunch of grapes, and dried fruits, like apricots.

5. Fill out spaces with edible garnish, like orange slices.

6. Add crackers or sliced baguette.

Set a Table the Fancy Way

Antiquated as proper place settings may seem, they still look lovely for nicer events. Here are the American rules:

- Plate in the center.
- Napkin to the left of the plate.
- Dinner fork on the napkin.
- Salad fork to the left of the dinner fork.
- Knife to the right of the plate.
- Soup spoon to the right of the knife.
- Water glass above and to the right of the plate.
- Wine glass above and to the right of the water glass.
- Salad plate, then soup bowl, stacked on the dinner plate.
- Dessert spoon horizontally above the plate.
- Place card above that.

Have Kids Set the Table

Use markers and paper to create a placemat depicting the proper arrangement of the plate, cup, and so on, then laminate it. The visual will help kids practice setting their own place.

Prep Your Food Safely

It's the boring side of cooking, and it's easy to ignore. But if you don't think about food safety, you might regret it. Here are some ways to prevent common cooking calamities:

- Wash your hands.
- Keep surfaces clean, especially when meat is involved. Keep raw and cooked meats apart by using different utensils and cutting boards and washing your hands frequently.
- Wash and rinse fruits and vegetables thoroughly before you eat them.
- When handling hot peppers, always wash your hands afterward. And here's a safety hack for very hot peppers: Poke your knife through the corner of a plastic bag and keep the handle of the knife (and thus your hand) inside the bag as you chop. Slide your other hand into another plastic bag to hold the pepper.
- Squeezing limes or lemons in the sunshine (mmm, margaritas) can cause a potentially serious skin condition that will ruin your vacay. So wash your skin with soap and water after dealing with those citrus fruits.

Look Past Expiration Dates

Weird as it can feel to eat food once the date stamped on it has passed, it's usually perfectly safe. Sell-by dates on food packaging are intended for store employees who stock the shelves, not for customers who eat the food. If the item has a "use by" or "best if used by" date, it probably won't go bad after that; it will simply dry out or lose freshness or flavor. Foods with a true expiration date include things like yeast, which simply might not do its job of raising your dough after a certain time has passed.

So how do you know when *not* to eat something? If it smells bad or strange, if it has visible mold or discoloration or just looks unusual to you, if its packaging is damaged, or if it's been cooked and left out too long (even if it looks fine), it's better to be safe than sorry.

The Lowdown on Mold

Ah, the eternal debate. Can you just cut the moldy part off and eat the rest, or does that tinge of blue indicate an invisible peril lurking throughout the food?

Because mold can cause serious health problems, most foods should be thrown away if you spot even a little bit of mold on them. Exceptions are firm fruits and vegetables (like carrots) and hard cheeses, which are okay to eat once the moldy area has been fully cut off. Cheeses made with mold, like Brie, are safe to eat unless they contain a mold that's not part of the manufacturing process.

Don't Put Hot Food in the Fridge

Did you ever get the general idea that you shouldn't put hot food straight into the fridge but didn't know why? Turns out, it's less about the risk to the newly cooked food (which can, in fact, be refrigerated quickly, though multiple small containers are better than one big pot) and more about the foods already in your fridge. The introduction of something steaming can raise the fridge temperature, making bacteria more apt to grow on refrigerated items. So let food cool a bit before putting it in the fridge.

Ask about Allergies

It seems every group includes at least a few people who can't eat a few things. And if you want to be a considerate host, you should ask your guests about dietary restrictions. However, this doesn't mean you have to cook ten different meals. First, listen to your guests. Some might be perfectly happy to come to your backyard party and have only a drink. Others will be totally fine eating some parts of the meal but not all or would simply prefer the dressing on the side. Some may need to bring their own food or eat beforehand.

Just remember that they're (hopefully) coming to see you, not your lasagna, delicious though it no doubt is.

Make Super Simple Pickles

If you finish a jar of pickles (or pickled anything) that you loved the flavor of, don't just pour out the remaining liquid. Instead, slice up a fresh cucumber (or other vegetables) and place them in the jar to make super easy instant "pickles" of your own. (Note: This isn't technically pickling, so your veggies won't last long. But you can enjoy them for the next several days.)

10 Recipe-Saving Substitutions

No matter what you're out of, there's something that can fill in:

1. No buttermilk? Substitute with 1 cup milk plus 1 tablespoon lemon juice or white vinegar.

2. No sour cream? Use plain yogurt.

3. No alcohol? In baking, you can swap booze for juice. In cooking, substitute nonalcoholic wine or beer for their alcoholic counterparts.

4. No bread crumbs? Use crumbled unsalted crackers.

5. No eggs? Substitute mashed bananas or applesauce in baking (use 3 tablespoons per egg). Or make a flax egg (1 tablespoon ground flaxseed meal mixed with 3 tablespoons water).

6. No brown sugar? For every cup, use 1 cup white sugar plus 1 tablespoon light molasses.

7. No baking powder? 1 teaspoon = $\frac{1}{4}$ teaspoon baking soda plus $\frac{1}{2}$ teaspoon cream of tartar.

8. No chocolate? 1 ounce = 3 tablespoons cocoa powder mixed with 1 tablespoon vegetable oil.

9. No cream of tartar? 1 teaspoon = $\frac{1}{2}$ teaspoon white vinegar.

10. No fresh garlic? 1 clove = $\frac{1}{8}$ teaspoon garlic powder.

Wax Paper vs. Parchment vs. Aluminum Foil

Wondering when to use which roll?

- **Aluminum foil** is an (almost) all-purpose liner and cover for pans and trays in the oven, whether you're making cookies, chicken, or broccoli. It also works for grilling and is especially good for making little packets to cook fish. And, of course, it's super useful for storing food in the fridge. (But don't use it in the microwave!)
- **Parchment paper** has a nonstick coating and is great for lining cake tins, cookie sheets, and brownie pans so your food comes out of/off the pan or tray perfectly. It's also ideal for roasting veggies in the oven. Just don't use it in an oven above 425°F.
- **Wax paper** is coated with, you guessed it, (food-safe) wax, which means it generally can't go in the oven. But it's great if you're making candy or chocolate (think peppermint bark). It's also good for storing foods in layers.

Cook with Less Mess

Here's an advanced-level cleaning tip: Avoid cleaning up because you never made a mess in the first place. Whoa. Try these tips to make cleanup a breeze:

- To stop boiling pots from overflowing and splattering your stove, place a large wooden spoon across the top of the pot. Remove when you're ready to add food. Magic!
- When cutting soft canned foods, like tomatoes, use kitchen scissors to chop them inside the can rather than moving them (and their drips) onto your cutting board.
- Line baking sheets with aluminum foil. (Bonus tip: To cook preportioned meals, fold ridges into the foil to divide into sections.)
- Protect your phone from crumbs and spills by slipping the device into a plastic baggie. (You can still tap and scroll.)

Make Entertaining Simple with a Buffet

A safe, crowd-pleasing, and easy-on-the-host option for almost any kind of casual occasion is to present the food assembly-line style.

Letting guests assemble their own plates is great for family members with different dietary needs, friends with various preferences, and adventurous eaters who want to try a bunch of different options.

It's also ideal if you're feeding kids, some of whom may be in a "plain pasta good, mushrooms evil" stage.

This setup works whether you're doing sundaes, tacos, pizza, sandwiches, salads, and a bunch of other themes.

What to Bring If You Can't Cook

Need to bring a dish to Thanksgiving dinner, or just want to pull your weight at a potluck? Here's how to show up with minimal kitchen action:

- Dress up store-bought rolls. Melt a stick of butter and stir in 1 teaspoon Italian seasoning and ½ teaspoon garlic powder. Brush over the top of the rolls, then bake on a baking sheet at 400°F for 5 minutes.

- Arrange store-bought cheese slices neatly on a fancy appetizer plate.

- Bring drinks, whether it's a standard choice like wine, a more adventurous alcohol, or a nonalcoholic option.

- Bring something people always need but forget to buy enough of, like ice.

- Need to go straight from the grocery store to the party? Grab something nostalgic, like ice cream sandwiches. Though not homemade, anything that evokes childhood memories is usually a crowd-pleaser.

3 Ways to Transform a Store-Bought Cake

Oh yeah, I totally made this myself.

1. **Turn typical icing flowers into a unique design.** Remove flowers with a butter knife and place them in bowls divided by color. Remove the white icing piped around the cake and stir into colored icings. Dot pastel icings around your cake and use a bench scraper to smooth it into psychedelic swirls.

2. **DIY double-layer.** Remove decorations from one small and one large round store-bought cake. Trim the cardboard under the small cake so it doesn't stick out. Cut plastic smoothie straws just slightly taller than the large cake and stick them into the cake's center. Place the small cake on top and decorate as you like.

3. **Fix a bakery cake mistake.** Scrape and smooth smudged icing on the top and sides of the cake so only a thin layer remains. Refrigerate 1 hour. Make it all look intentional by adding chocolate ganache and fruit toppings.

Upgrade Your
PARTY
PUNCH

Punch is synonymous with parties. Here are two ways to transcend the traditional punch bowl image:

1. Make a **fun watermelon punch bowl**.

- Carefully cut the top off a watermelon and scoop out the innards.
- Blend with an immersion blender, then strain.
- Use an apple corer to cut a circular hole in the melon rind a few inches from the bottom.
- Insert a keg tap into the hole.
- Add ice to the melon bowl, followed by the juice. Stir in lime juice (and optional alcohol) and replace the "lid."

BLEND

2. Make a **frozen raspberry punch**.

- Place raspberries at the bottoms of muffin tin liners.
- Top with scoops of sherbet. Freeze.
- Add more fresh raspberries to a jug with 6 ounces fruit punch concentrate and 6 ounces pink lemonade concentrate. Add 5 cups ginger ale.
- Pop a sherbet ball into a Mason jar or large drinking glass, then fill with punch.

5 Ways to Get Kids to Eat Healthy

"Kid food" often conjures up images of processed, packaged treats. But kids can totally love healthy foods too. Here are some clever ways to introduce nutritious foods to children:

1. Blend grated veggies into patties along with meat.

2. Cut fruits into small pieces and stack them on wood skewers. Brush with honey for added sweetness.

3. Have kids write their favorite healthy mains and sides on three wooden block "dice." When it's time to make dinner, they can "roll" for, say, chicken with broccoli and potatoes.

4. Blend in chopped cauliflower, carrots, and squash as you cook cheese sauce for hidden vegetable mac and cheese.

5. If your kids are bored by vegetables, try downsizing and serve cute little versions. Pick the tiniest tomatoes, baby corn and carrots, fingerling potatoes, and mini-peppers and cucumbers.

Clean These Sneaky Kitchen Areas

Kitchens have their own special ways of getting gross. Check these spots while you're cleaning up:

- Handles of the oven, fridge, cabinets, drawers, and any other frequently grabbed place.
- Cabinet doors, including their edges.
- The exterior of the oven, fridge, and freezer. Including stuff that's on the fridge, like magnets.
- The dish drainer, including the tray underneath and the little cutlery basket.
- Under small appliances that always stand in the same place, like toasters and microwaves.
- Walls. Anywhere food is prepared, drips can end up in unexpected places.
- Sponges (replace often) and dish towels (throw in the wash).

Grow Greens in Your Kitchen

You don't need a yard to have a garden. Here's how to grow greens in even the tiniest apartment. Fill two rectangular planter boxes with soil. These can be small enough to fit on your counter—say, the size of a loaf of bread—as long as they can accommodate your veggies.

Take the leftover stem from a head of **lettuce** (cut it about 2 inches from the bottom). Place it in a glass with a small amount of water so that only the very bottom of the stem is submerged. When leaves begin to sprout, transfer it to the soil.

Do the same with a full stalk of **celery** (that means the whole bunch, not just one stick), transferring to the soil when new sticks begin growing.

Take three sprigs each of **mint and basil**. Trim 3 inches down from the top. Fill two glasses with about 1 inch of water and stand the herbs upright in them. When roots grow 2 inches, transfer them to the soil.

Chop about six **green onions** 2 inches from the bottom. Stand them up in a glass with just enough water to cover the roots. Transfer to the soil after 5–7 days.

5 Makeshift Kitchen Tools

Next time you're in a pinch, remember these clever maneuvers:

1. **Want to eat some tuna, but you can't find a can opener?** Rub the can upside down on pavement again and again, then use a spoon edge to coax the lid open.

2. **All beer bottle and no can opener?** Flip that cap with the edge of a spoon, the rounded part of a belt buckle, the tip of a key or flathead screwdriver, or the strike plate on a door.

3. **Baking bread and realize at the worst moment that you're rolling pin-less?** Use a bottle instead.

4. **Jar with a stuck lid, and you don't have a gadget to pop it?** Use the rubber glove you wear to wash dishes.

5. **Need to soften butter ASAP without a microwave?** Heat a drinking glass by putting warm liquid in it, then dump the liquid and place the cup upside down over the butter on a plate.

4 Fruits You've Been Eating Wrong

Well, not *wrong* exactly. But maybe there's a better way:

1. Don't peel that **kiwi**. Just scoop it out of its skin with a spoon.

2. Peel **bananas** from the bottom. It's easier, the stem is now a handle, and monkeys do it that way.

3. Make **watermelon** easy by cutting the melon in half. Place one half cut side down and make slices 1–2 inches wide. Now slice the opposite way, creating squares, or watermelon sticks.

4. To peel a **peach**, place it in hot water for 20 seconds, transfer it to an ice water bath for 10 seconds, and gently pull skin off with your hands. (The same method works with tomatoes—just score an X on the bottom first [start peeling from here] and give them 45 seconds in the hot bath.)

Reuse Kitchen Scraps

Composting is a great way to get rid of kitchen leftovers. But there are other ways to reuse odds and ends too:

- Use eggshells along with soap and water to scrub pots and pans. The shells help release sticky, burnt-on messes.
- Place herb stems (e.g., rosemary, thyme, parsley) in an airtight container. Cover with olive oil and let sit at least a week. Presto: infused oil for dipping, cooking, or dressings.
- Let used tea bags dry completely. Stick in smelly shoes and let sit overnight to absorb odors.
- Use peeled cucumber skin ribbons to gently flavor a tall glass of ice water. Bonus: It's super pretty!
- Take coffee grounds from the filter and let dry completely in a firesafe bowl. Then bring them outside and burn them with a lighter. The smoke from the smoldering grounds will help repel insects.

Cook for One

Here's how to make the most of solo shopping and cooking:

- Split recipes in half or quarters before you cook. Split leftovers into portioned servings.
- Freeze uncooked foods (like ground beef or turkey) split into servings, and embrace bags of frozen vegetables, which last a long time and can be cooked a little at a time.
- Don't feel tied to recipes. You don't need to impress anyone but yourself, so if you want to just cook up a variety of tasty things, go for it.

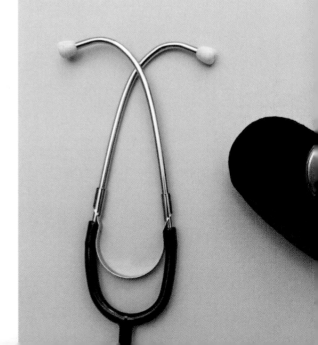

CHAPTER

5

Beauty & Wellness

STAY FRESH-FACED AND WELL-RESTED

Health, skin care, self-care: They're parts of maintaining your physical and mental self, and they come wIth confusing buzzwords, trends, and hashtags. This chapter aims to simplify **wellness**. It's got DIYs for at-home spa days and routine maintenance, advice for fitting **self-care** into your busy life, and fun hacks on workouts and sleep.

   None of this info is a routine that you *have* to follow. Instead, it's a reminder to find what works for you and uncomplicate the process of wellness.

New Year, New You?

Want to make some life changes? Making resolutions can help—if they're created with the right mindset and approach. Here's how to make better resolutions:

- You don't have to tie your resolution to the new year or any particular day. But it can help to associate a change with a birthday, a new season, a new month, a Monday, or a significant date.
- Make specific and short-term resolutions. "Get in shape" feels insurmountable; "walk for X minutes per day this month" feels doable.
- Don't make multiple resolutions at once. Start with something small *or* with one big thing that will positively affect multiple aspects of your life.
- Find a meaningful quote, image, or song to motivate, remind, and reassure you along your journey.
- Don't worry if resolutions just don't work for you. There are plenty of other methods to drop a bad habit or start working toward a goal!

Adopt These Simple Preventative Wellness Practices

Because when you're old, you'll either be mad you didn't do this stuff—or so thankful you did.

- Care for your teeth by going to the dentist and brushing and flossing at home.
- Schedule regular checkups at the doctor and keep up with stuff like tetanus shots.
- Get unusual symptoms checked out (and not just by the Internet).
- Do some kind of regular physical activity.
- Eat more healthy, nutritious foods. Even if you eat other, less healthy stuff too.
- Wear proper clothes, supportive footwear, and protective gear when necessary.

Start—and Keep—a Wellness Habit

The tiniest life changes can be the hardest to implement, but there is an easy way to permanently add those little habits into your life: Something called habit stacking or habit chaining. There's a scientific explanation for how it trains your brain, but, simply put, it's easier to do a thing when it consistently accompanies another thing you're already doing. Start applying sunscreen right after brushing your teeth in the morning (you're doing that, right?), and soon the two behaviors will become equally automatic.

Small Changes FTW

We all love a dramatic transformation, a rock-bottom turnaround, a glow-up with a soundtrack. But that kind of change doesn't work for everyone, and often, that expectation can set you up to fail. It's just as valid and sometimes more effective to make little, incremental changes. Say you want to kick a caffeine addiction. Rather than quitting coffee cold turkey and suffering the headaches and tiredness, wean yourself off slowly. Switch to 75 percent caf, 25 percent decaf for a week or two. Then go 50/50. Then 25/75. And so on.

Write Your User Manual

Because everyone is different, much of adulthood is figuring yourself out. From big things, like whether you're introverted, extroverted, or in-between, to little things, like whether you like cilantro.

Figuring this out is a lifelong process. And remembering it all is another thing. So consider compiling a literal document, a sort of instruction sheet for your own care and feeding. You can also create some specific troubleshooting pages, such as what to do when you're burned out, what makes you feel better when you're feeling sad, or how to reset after a vacation or especially stressful period at work.

Get Your Checkups

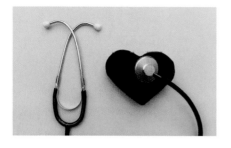

When you were a kid, your parents or guardians probably scheduled stuff like doctor's appointments for you. But now that it's up to you, is it getting done regularly? Going to the doctor and dentist regularly, getting routine screenings, and checking out any new or worrisome symptoms is part of being a healthy, responsible adult. Is it the most fun thing ever? No. But you have to do it. Because this book told you to.

8 Ways to Feel Better Fast

When you feel off, having some proven mood boosters in the back of your mind—or jotted down—means you don't have to come up with solutions every time. Here are some common mood lifters that might resonate with you:

1. Listen to a happy or calming playlist.

2. Do some kind of physical movement.

3. Get outside.

4. Call or text a friend.

5. Play with a pet.

6. Take a nap.

7. Eat or drink something good.

8. Shower or wash your face.

Go Green (Tea)

Green tea has long been renowned for its health benefits, and its trendier cousin, matcha, is currently having a moment. Green tea's antioxidant, anti-inflammatory, and antimicrobial properties also make it ideal for DIY skin remedies. A green tea bag can be used as a warm or cold compress for puffy eyes; mixed with an equal amount of honey to create a face mask to treat acne; or steeped, cooled, and put in a spray bottle to spritz on inflamed skin.

Stock Basic First Aid Supplies

Hopefully, you won't need them. But if you do, you'll be glad you had them at the ready:

- Bandages in various shapes/sizes
- Gauze pads or rolls
- Surgical tape
- Rubbing alcohol
- Surgical masks
- Disposable gloves
- Antiseptic wipes
- Thermometer

- Hydrogen peroxide
- Hydrocortisone cream
- Antibiotic ointment
- Tweezers
- Allergy pills (e.g., Benadryl or Claritin)
- Antihistamines

- OTC pain relievers (e.g., acetaminophen or ibuprofen)
- Aspirin
- Ice packs
- A heating pad (or instant heat packs)

Kitchen Skin Care

Did you know some of your favorite foods are leading double lives as skincare products?

- Apply egg whites as a face mask for 10–20 minutes to fight acne-causing bacteria and temporarily tighten skin. Use egg yolks (leave on for 5–10 minutes) to hydrate dry or flaky skin. Rinse off when done.
- Apply honey as a mask or spot treatment to help balance skin affected by acne, eczema, or psoriasis.
- It's a cliché stock photo for a reason: Placing cucumber slices over your eyelids really does cool and depuff. Or use cucumber water to wash or spritz your face for added refreshment.
- Don't let your toast have all the avocados because they're also a skin moisturizer, nourisher, and inflammation fighter. Avocados may also help heal wounds and prevent acne. Spread on skin for 10–15 minutes then rinse off.

Make Your Own Natural Lip Balm

Have you ever stopped to think about how much lip balm you've used over your lifetime? Don't you want to make your own all-natural lip balm now? Here's how: Heat an inch of water in a small pot on medium heat. Rest a glass bowl on the pot, creating a double boiler effect. Melt 1 tablespoon of beeswax, 2 tablespoons of shea butter, and 2 tablespoons of coconut oil in the bowl. Remove from heat and add about 20 drops of peppermint essential oil. Before the mixture starts to harden, pour into small containers (this recipe makes about twelve typically sized lip balms) and let them harden with the lids off.

Salve for Tattoos & Scrapes

Soothe your skin with a self-made salve that's all natural. Pour 1 cup coconut oil into a double boiler. Add 1 cup of plantago leaf. (Search online for this ingredient.) Stir. Heat on low for 48–72 hours. (Turn off overnight or when you can't be nearby.) Strain into a bowl, then return the oil to the double boiler, heating on low. Add 10 drops of eucalyptus essential oil and 8 teaspoons of organic beeswax. Stir until the beeswax dissolves, then pour into a glass jar. Let harden into a balm texture. Apply to minor burns or new tats.

Bath Salts

Stir up this fun recipe for a rainbow of soothing salts. Divide a package of Epsom salts into three equal parts. To one of them, add 5 drops of essential oil. Add several drops of food coloring in the color of your choice. Stir with a spoon. Repeat twice more using two separate bowls and different colors for the remaining two-thirds of the package of Epsom salts. Pour the three mixtures into an airtight glass jar in alternating layers. Next time you bathe, scoop some of the mix into the water, following the directions for use on the package of Epsom salts.

Beard Oil DIY

Smooth this solution on your beard to moisturize hair (and feel extra dapper while you're at it). Mix $\frac{1}{2}$ ounce of jojoba oil, $\frac{1}{2}$ ounce of almond oil, 12 drops of tea tree oil, and 12 drops of rosemary oil in a small bowl. Pour into a small dropper bottle. (Use a funnel for easier pouring.) Shake well. Apply 2–4 drops for a softer beard.

All-Natural Shaving Cream DIY

Making your own shaving cream gives you control over the ingredients, scent (or lack thereof), and moisture levels. Melt $\frac{2}{3}$ cup of coconut oil and $\frac{2}{3}$ cup of shea butter lotion in a pot on medium heat and stir. Add $\frac{1}{4}$ cup of olive oil, then $\frac{1}{4}$ cup of castile soap. (Optional: Add $\frac{1}{2}$ teaspoon of vitamin E oil for extra moisturizing power and $\frac{1}{2}$ teaspoon of essential oil for scent.) Cook on medium heat, stirring to combine. Refrigerate in a bowl for 60 minutes or until solid. Whip for 3–4 minutes with a hand mixer until light and fluffy. Put in a container and store in a cool place.

Face Masks DIY

Whether your skin needs refreshing or soothing, you can mix up your own mask instead of purchasing one:

- **Charcoal face mask:** Mix $\frac{1}{4}$ cup apple cider vinegar and $\frac{1}{8}$ cup aloe vera gel. Gradually add $\frac{1}{3}$ cup bentonite clay powder and stir. Add 5 drops tea tree oil. Add the contents of five charcoal capsules and stir. Apply to face for 10–15 minutes, then rinse off.
- **Mint oatmeal honey face mask:** Blend a few mint leaves with $\frac{1}{3}$ cup uncooked rolled oats. Then add 2 tablespoons water and 2 tablespoons honey and blend. Apply to face for 10–15 minutes, then rinse off. Keep mixtures refrigerated and use within 2 days.

Actually Enjoy Exercise

Unless you're extraordinarily motivated (or perhaps paid) to do it, the only way to maintain an exercise habit over time is to find a type of physical movement you really enjoy. That activity doesn't have to stay the same over your lifetime or even throughout the year or month. It can be gentle, like walking or stretching. It can be done in a group or solo. But it has to be something you like doing—or at the very least, strongly like having done—or you will not keep it up.

5 Activities to Try If You "Hate Working Out"

Gyms, classes, weights, timers, teams, coaches, trainers, Lycra. If these are your least favorite words, don't worry, there are hundreds of other ways you can get the benefits of exercise. Here are five:

1. Walking: Around your neighborhood, around a different and therefore more interesting neighborhood, on a walking path in a park, or literally anywhere that's safe to stroll.

2. Hiking: It doesn't have to be super strenuous (though that's awesome too). Much of what's called "hiking" is just walking along a trail. So don't be intimidated by hikes in state or national parks or nature preserves—just check the difficulty level if you're new to outdoorsy life.

3. Dancing: In the club, in the kitchen, whatever works.

4. Stretching: Start slow and gentle (maybe follow some beginner instructional videos) and relax those tense muscles. Get a cheap yoga mat so it's more comfortable to do floor stretches.

5. Learning a skill or achieving a goal: Think indoor wall climbing, pole dancing, skateboarding, roller-skating, or anything that feels exciting enough to get you out of the house.

Improve Your Home Workout

Working out at home is great: You can do it at any hour, there's no one around to judge you, and you can blast your music. But if it's inconvenient, you're less likely to do it. Here's how to make your space more fitness-friendly:

- Use a lidded ottoman as stealthy storage for weights or exercise bands.
- Keep clean towels nearby (roll them up in linen bins to feel fancy).
- Stash flat or rolled equipment, like yoga mats or interlocking foam floor tiles, behind a couch or in a closet. (Keep wipes nearby to disinfect after use.)
- If home workouts become a permanent part of your life, consider turning a room or corner into a gym area.

Upgrade Your Gym Trips

Take your gym routine up a notch with these easy hacks to make your exercise routine easier and more enjoyable:

- Fill your reusable water bottle halfway. Screw the lid on and freeze the bottle lying sideways. Before you leave, fill the other half with water. Perfectly cold water bottle!
- Prevent smelly sneakers post-workout. Place both shoes in a plastic shower cap, soles down, and stick an unused tea bag in each.
- Don't lug big bottles of face soap, moisturizer, shampoo, and conditioner into the gym shower. Bring the perfect amount of product by decanting a dollop into each half of a contact lens case.
- Prepare a super soothing washcloth by dipping it in a bowl of water mixed with a couple drops eucalyptus oil. Store in the fridge and stick in a plastic baggie for easy transport.
- Stash dryer sheets in your gym bag to keep it smelling fresh.

8 Tips to Help You Sleep

You know sleep is important. But knowing and doing are very different things, especially when actually falling—and staying—asleep is so hard sometimes. Here are some little changes to make for better sleep:

1. Avoid alcohol. (It might make you sleepy, but it will mess up the quality of your sleep throughout the night.)

2. Exercise daily (but stop 2–3 hours before bed).

3. Get computers, work materials, and the TV or tablet out of your bedroom.

4. Make your bed every morning.

5. Go to bed and wake up at the same time every day.

6. Practice slowly breathing in, holding, and then breathing out to slow down and unwind.

7. Try progressive muscle relaxation: Tense each muscle group for about 20 seconds, then release.

8. Gently massage your jawline, temples, forehead, neck, and skull with two fingers of each hand to release tension.

Beyond Beauty Sleep

There's always that person who brags, "I'll sleep when I'm dead!" to justify their fast-paced lifestyle. But the benefits of proper sleep are too important to ignore, and going too long without sleep can dramatically derail your mood and even your health. (It's dangerous too. Driving while sleepy, for instance, can be as deadly as driving while intoxicated.) Sleeping well can help your body fight off illness and stay healthy as you age, as well as keeping your mind sharp and reducing stress on a daily basis.

That's why sleep hygiene (which means healthy habits around sleep, not cleanliness, though it's always good to be clean) is crucial to wellness.

Even if you're in your twenties, when most people can get away with all-nighters and unpredictable sleep schedules, it's good to know that this will almost certainly change as you grow older, so it's not a bad idea to start incorporating good sleep habits now.

5 Ways (Besides Caffeine) to Wake Up Fast

Yeah, yeah, you should get a good night's sleep. But sometimes, for whatever reason, you simply don't. And you still need to wake up and go to work or take care of kids or do something other than lounge around bingeing whole seasons of TV shows. Here are some tips for when coffee isn't cutting it:

1. Store a face roller in the freezer and use it to depuff and perk up.

2. Shower (and wash your hair if possible).

3. Take a quick walk outside; if you can't go out, do some stretches or other light physical activity.

4. Find a go-to song or create a whole playlist of music that gets you going.

5. Throw yourself into a task. Sometimes jumping in and doing one small action (like paying a bill or taking out the garbage) engages the "awake stuff" part of your brain.

2 Fixes for Common Makeup Mishaps

When you inadvertently destroy your lipstick or blush (especially if it cost an embarrassing amount of money), it's a special kind of sadness. But it can be fixed!

1. Restore a shattered powder by mixing the remaining product in its compact with a few drops rubbing alcohol. Smooth it with the back of a spoon, then wait 1 hour. Use a cotton swab to clean up any spills, then place a paper towel over the powder and pack the makeup into place with the cap of a bottle.

2. Repair a broken lipstick by heating the bottom half (still in the tube) with a lighter. When it's soft, place the broken-off bit back on, and use the lighter to heat the new seam. While it's still melty, roll the lipstick down and clean up the case.

Make Your Own Matcha Face Mask

Matcha provides all the benefits of green tea, and stirring it into a face mask delivers those benefits straight to your skin. Best of all, it's super easy to make. Stir 3 teaspoons matcha powder (it has anti-inflammatory and antioxidant properties) with 1½ teaspoons coconut oil (which is both antiseptic and moisturizing) and 1½ teaspoons water. Apply to skin right away and leave on for about 10 minutes, then rinse. You can also store it for up to 1 week.

Makeup Remover

Why buy fancy (and pricey) makeup removers when you can make one at home from simple ingredients? To do it, just stir together 2 tablespoons of baby shampoo, 2 tablespoons of coconut oil, and 1 cup of purified water. Then fill a small glass jar with a stack of cotton pads. Pour your liquid in to cover and saturate the pads, and place a lid on the container.

Makeup Setting Spray

The streaky, melty makeup look is no fun. Keep your makeup in its place with this easy concoction. Stir 3 tablespoons of water, 1 tablespoon of witch hazel, 1 tablespoon of aloe vera, and 6 drops of lavender oil in a bowl. Then pour into a spray bottle and aim at your face.

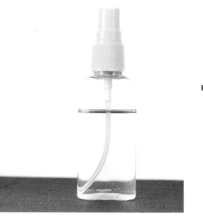

Sage & Rosemary Face Toner

You'll feel at one with nature when you spray this refreshing herbal toner on your skin. Snip a few leaves of sage and sprigs of rosemary and add them to a small pot with ¼ cup of water. Bring to a boil, then remove from heat and let steep for 1 hour. Pour 1 tablespoon of witch hazel and ½ teaspoon of vegetable glycerin into a glass bowl. Strain the sage and rosemary liquid into the bowl. Pour into a small spray bottle.

Check In with Yourself

Feeling down but don't know why? Here's a checklist of common culprits:

- Are you too hot or too cold?
- Are you thirsty, tired, hungry, or hungover?
- Is something in your environment or surroundings bothering you?
- Are you coming down with a cold or other illness?
- Do you need caffeine (if you typically drink caffeine)?
- Have you had too much of some food that's been known to make you feel wired/tired/weird before?
- Are you stressed or worried about a situation?
- Did you remember or watch something unpleasant?
- Did someone violate a boundary (even unintentionally)?
- Did something sad happen to you or someone you know, or did you hear about something sad on the news?
- Are you angry about something in your life or the world?

Wellness: Not One Size Fits All

Sometimes health advice is universal (e.g., cover your mouth when you cough). Often it's not (e.g., nuts are a great source of healthy fats...unless you're allergic to them). Many people (and corporations) will tell you to get X hours of sleep, eat Y number of calories, meditate, jog, drink mushroom tea, and on and on. And all of these may be fine advice for someone—but they can't all apply to everyone. So in this world of conflicting claims, you have to figure out which rules apply to you.

How to Organize for Mental Calm

Living in an organized space is really good for your mental clarity. It also turns out that even the process of organizing itself can help you feel more in control, productive, and generally in charge of your life—thus improving your mental health. Try one of these organizing projects to calm your frenzied brain:

- Sort out your wardrobe.
- Rearrange things to create a cozy, safe space, like a reading nook.
- Organize a room to give yourself a hobby space. Make your kitchen enjoyable to cook in, set up a little art studio corner in the living room, or do some gardening, outside or in.
- Declutter a piece of your past. This can be emotional but will feel so worth it.
- Organize something you love and feel close to, like a book collection or old photos.

Quit Unnecessary Self-Care

A lot of self-care, even when it comes under the umbrella of "relaxation," sounds suspiciously like work. Someone's always exhorting you to add something to your routine or read a stack of self-help books. Instead, try some of these ideas to treat yourself without exerting too much effort:

- Drop a hobby or activity that doesn't fulfill you.
- Delete a step from your routine. If some aspect of your regimen hasn't clicked for you, eliminate it.
- Sleep and rest more! Stay in bed later, go to bed earlier, or take a restful break during the day.
- Indulge in a pastime you abandoned because it wasn't "productive."
- Find a way to simplify or automate a regular, necessary chore.

Make Your Own COLD REMEDIES

Feeling sneezy, dopey, grumpy, and sleepy? These home remedies will make you happy:

- **Healing soak:** Mix ½ cup baking soda, 1 cup Epsom salts, and a few drops peppermint oil, eucalyptus oil, and tea tree oil. Scoop into your bath.

- **Muscle soother:** Fill a cotton sock halfway with uncooked rice. Stir in a drop of peppermint oil and eucalyptus oil. Tie the sock closed. Microwave for 2 minutes, then place on skin to soothe aches.

- **Anti-inflammatory tea:** Heat 1 cup water, 1 teaspoon ground turmeric, 1 inch sliced ginger, and 1 teaspoon honey on the stovetop. Strain, add a squeeze of lemon, and sip to soothe a sore throat.

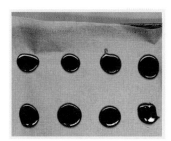

- **Cough drops:** Boil ¾ cup water with sliced ginger and one tea bag each of peppermint and chamomile tea. Strain, then add ¾ cup honey. Boil to 300°F. Drop onto a parchment-lined baking sheet and cool for 1 hour.

DIY

Take a Day Off

Have you ever been slogging through some task at work, feeling like it's just impossible, and then you happen to take the following day off, and when you come back, your impossible task is magically pretty effortless? That phenomenon is a real thing!

Taking a day off (from work or from other responsibilities) and giving yourself permission to stop thinking about whatever you're "supposed to be" thinking about can actually make you more productive.

So if you're feeling overwhelmed—even if you're busy, even if you have a to-do list longer than a city bus, even if you feel guilty or scared you won't catch up—take a day off if you can.

Enjoy Time in Nature

View it through the lens of science, spirituality, art, or all of the above, it can't be denied: Being outside is good for your mind, body, and spirit. (General time spent in nature, that is, not poison ivy and rattlesnakes.) Luckily, there are numerous ways to get out into nature or bring nature to you.

Go for a walk in the woods or along the beach or riverfront. Wander through a city park or sit on a bench observing the birds and squirrels. Visit a flower farm, garden, greenhouse, pond, or anywhere—wild or cultivated—you can immerse yourself in natural beauty. Take up a hobby, like hiking or gardening, that encourages you to get outside.

And when you can't get out, take a few minutes to watch the sunrise or sunset, open the window, breathe the air, or just let the sun (or the rain) hit your face.

Try a Digital Detox

Devices are such a big part of our lives (read: practically surgically attached to our hands) that going without them can feel like detaching from civilization. But whether you vaguely recall a time when your phone didn't give you driving directions or the in-app purchase life is all you've ever known, it's worth taking an occasional break.

It could be a day, a weekend, or a long vacation in the remote Wi-Fi-less wilderness. It could just mean setting the phone aside for the first few hours of your morning or the hours before bed.

And you can choose which aspects of being online drain your time and energy. Maybe you need to step away from social media, emails and texts, or news updates. Or maybe you'd benefit from a day without any electronics in your life. Experiment and reflect on how you feel when you temporarily remove those options.

To Count or Not to Count (Steps)

It seems like everyone's trying to get their 10,000 steps in. But do you really have to? Well, it turns out that 10K is an arbitrary number, invented for a Japanese marketing campaign in the 1960s. But research has found that walking more (i.e., leading an active life and avoiding being sedentary) does improve your health and longevity. So while there's no need to obsess over a specific number of steps—10,000 is cool, 8,000 is cool, 5,000 is a lot better than 850—there's no need to fixate on that particular number. If keeping count helps you, great, and if not, just, you know, try to walk a lot.

Make Your Own Rosemary Mint Shampoo

Rosemary is an antioxidant and antibacterial; mint stimulates the scalp—and both smell yummy. Sounds like a great combo for a homemade shampoo! Here's how to make it:

Add a couple sprigs of rosemary and mint to a small pot with $\frac{1}{2}$ cup unsweetened shredded coconut and 1 cup water. Heat and stir, then let simmer for 30 minutes. Use cheesecloth and a strainer to squeeze the resulting liquid into a bowl. Pour 1 cup castile soap into a pump-top bottle. (Add 1 teaspoon almond oil if you have a dry scalp.) Finally, add your rosemary mixture and shake.

Drink Water

This is one of those pieces of advice you hear all the time—but that's because it's tried and true. Over the years, various amounts in different units of measurement have had their moment as the supposedly magic number. (8 glasses! A gallon! 2 liters!) Of course, your body isn't counting ounces, but it does need hydration—and quite possibly more than you're currently getting. Drinking enough water helps your digestion, your skin, and even your mood and energy levels. So especially if you're feeling a little "blah" lately and don't quite know why, make sure you're drinking a decent amount of water and see if that perks you up.

How to Hydrate If You Don't Like Water

What if you *whispers* just dislike drinking water? Here's how to hydrate with nonbasic water options:

- Flavor your water with lemon, cucumber, or fruit.
- Try it with ice. Some people don't like their H_2O at room temp but love it on the rocks.
- Drink herbal tea.
- Dilute fruit juice with water.
- Eat plenty of water-rich foods. (Watermelon and cucumber are good options.)
- Try a filter. Some tap water has a taste that goes away when run through a pitcher filter.

Deal with the Heat

Whether you love three-digit temps or eagerly await sweater weather, you should be aware of the little adjustments that can help you stay healthy in the heat. Here's what to do when it's really hot:

- **Drink enough fluids.**
- **Protect your skin and hair with sunscreen and soothing products.** Don't hesitate to wear a hat or swimming cap, or to cover more skin, if you tend to be sensitive. Heat and humidity can be harsh, as can the sea and swimming pool.
- **Don't completely shun the sun.** Vitamin D and sunlight itself are good for you—just try to get it at the beginning or end of the day instead of from the superstrong midday sun.
- **Make use of mornings.** Do exercise and yard work early in the day.
- **Fan yourself.** Especially if you don't have AC, a humble fan can do a lot to cool you down.
- **Chill out.** Suck on some ice cubes, freeze juices in pop molds, eat fruit, and cool yourself with damp washcloths.

Stay Warm

What's worse than Mercury in retrograde? Mercury falling on the thermometer. It's easy to feel miserable when it's cold out, especially since that chill often comes with darkness and bad weather! Get cozier with these tips:

- Drink warm liquids and eat hot foods.
- See if using more spices in cooking warms you up.
- Cover any exposed skin when you go outside. A flash of ankle is no longer scandalous, but can let a surprising amount of cold air in under your clothes.
- Move! (Anyone who's shoveled knows how quickly you can heat up even in the most frigid of conditions.)

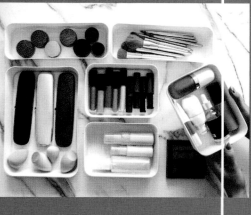

6 Fun Wellness Upgrades

It might sound silly, but elevating mundane wellness practices in the tiniest of ways can improve your daily life.

1. Trade your basic skin-colored bandages for ones in bold colors, pretty patterns, or whimsical designs. Are these meant for kids? Perhaps. Do they cover adult cuts and scrapes just as well? Definitely.

2. Invest in comfortable workout clothes and shoes you actually really like.

3. Get a really nice, functional, and attractive reusable water bottle.

4. Make your bed with sheets, blankets, and pillows that make you feel amazing when you lie down.

5. If you're a fan of old-school notebooks, planners, and pens, find ones you love so much you'll look forward to using them every day.

6. Implement a neat and effective storage system for beauty and health products. You'll be more likely to paint your nails and take your vitamins if you don't have to rummage through a messy drawer to find them.

Declutter Your Skin Care

From double-cleansing to ten-step routines, it's easy to accumulate a lot of skincare products. But chances are you'll save cash, time, and quite possibly your actual skin if you embrace a more streamlined regimen. Serious skin issues often require a dermatologist; less critical but nevertheless annoying problems are more often solved by removing something (be it a product, food, or habit) than adding it.

Think of Self-Care As Self-Compassion

The concept of self-care, as presented in pop culture, sometimes feels like a punishment (Early morning workouts! Biohacking! Relentless self-improvement!) and other times like self-indulgence (But first, wine!). It's a bit disorienting TBH. Like, is self-care cake and pedicures or 10Ks and supplement shakes?

Here's an easier way to think about caring for yourself. Imagine how you'd treat a beloved pet. If your cat needed medication, you'd give it to her, right? You wouldn't feed her unhealthy treats every day, but you would feed her nutritious food while letting her enjoy a treat occasionally. And you wouldn't shame her for being afraid of the vacuum cleaner.

You can look out for your physical, mental, and emotional well-being in the same way. In other words, it's all about balancing compassion and discipline, incorporating some early morning workouts and some glasses of wine along the way.

5 Beauty Products That Do Double Duty

You multitask; so can your makeup! These products are among the most versatile:

1. Lipstick: Don't let anyone tell you it's not also blush, eyeshadow, or even—depending on the shade—highlighter or bronzer. Same goes for gloss, tint, and any other lip product.

2. Hair conditioner: If you don't have shaving cream, conditioner is a handy replacement.

3. Foaming hand soap: Breaking news: It's body wash too.

4. Brow, lip, or eyeliner pencils: Branding aside, these are interchangeable. (But sanitize any would-be eye pencil with rubbing alcohol first!)

5. Petroleum jelly: It's not just a lip balm and salve for minor scrapes. It can also step in when you're out of eye makeup remover, cuticle oil, or brow gel. It can also smooth flyaway hairs around your brow, moisturize your face and hands, and work as an overnight treatment for rough skin on elbows and feet.

Stretch Your Beauty Products

Try these tricks to stop wasting what feels like one-fourth of your favorite products:

- When bar soaps get too tiny to handle comfortably, meld them together by wetting and frothing up with your hands a few times.
- Slice tubes with scissors about an inch above the opening and scoop out the product hiding within. Or buy a tool made to help you squeeze the last drop from a tube.
- Revive that last bit of drying mascara by adding a couple eye drops into the tube.
- Add a little water to shampoo and conditioner bottles and shake to free up the dregs.

Promote Wellness with a Clean Bathroom

Decluttering your bathroom cupboards and medicine cabinet—as well as any other places where you store beauty and health products—makes you feel good in the moment *and* helps you stay healthy in the future.

- Safely dispose of expired medications, both prescription and OTC.
- Check products for a stamped expiration date or little jar symbol indicating the product's life span in months.
- Go through makeup and junk anything that looks or smells funny or that you don't use.
- Wash makeup brushes and replace old sponge applicators and mascara wands.
- Get rid of unused soaps, shampoos, or lotions.
- Trade your toothbrush for a fresh one.

Reap All the Benefits of Aloe Vera

Aloe vera is one spiky plant you *do* want to get your hands on. The clear gel contained within this succulent's spiky leaves is gentle yet powerful, boasting a bevy of beauty benefits.

You can use aloe to soothe sunburned skin, minor burns, scrapes, and cuts. It's also an effective moisturizer for both oily and dry skin types, and it may minimize dark spots. Aloe can help calm skin conditions like eczema, psoriasis, and acne, and it's said to be good for the hair and scalp as well.

The plant itself is kinda cool-looking and pretty hard to kill, so while you can buy the gel bottled, often mixed with additional skin soothers, you may prefer to go natural and just keep this little green friend in your home.

Embrace Lists

Much of wellness is mental, and just like your closet, your brain needs to be decluttered sometimes. Making lists is an easy way to sort out the stuff in your mind, clear out what doesn't need to be there anymore, and get the rest in order. You can make lists of pretty much anything:

- Tasks you need to do today or this week.
- Experiences you want to have someday.
- Hopes and dreams.
- Stuff you're stressing over.

- Phone calls and appointments you need to make.
- Ideas for creative projects.
- TV shows you want to watch.
- Goals you want to accomplish.

Getting it out of your head and on paper (or a notes app) makes it easier to let unimportant stuff go and take action on necessary stuff.

Be Conscious of Your Personal Environment

Feeling run-down, congested, or achy? It might not be you; it might be your environment. Think about potential allergens, like dust, pollen, or smoke, that you might be encountering at home, work, or anywhere you spend time. Is your space clean? Is it moldy? Is it too hot or cold? Do you get fresh air? All of those factors can really impact your physical well-being. In addition, factors like the firmness of your mattress or the height of your office chair could be affecting you in ways you'd never even think about.

You might not be able to change some of these things, at least not right away. But you can plan for future improvements, and you can control how you manage these everyday challenges.

8 Ways to Make Your Room Zen

Having a calm environment in which to chill is the best way to prepare for a busy week or unwind after a long day.

1. Embrace natural light. Hang curtains or blinds that let sunlight in.

2. Keep a soft throw blanket on your bed. Warm layers = max coziness.

3. Add plants. They'll help clean the air and look good doing it.

4. Keep a diffuser or scented candle in your room. Aromas can be calming.

5. Hang string lights. Warm lights are soothing.

6. Decorate with photos of family and friends or mementos that evoke connection and happy thoughts.

7. Keep your space clean and free of clutter. (It helps you feel in control.)

8. Dust regularly to improve air quality.

Try Journaling

Journaling can help you plan your days, express your creativity, or clarify your thoughts. But writing endless lines of prose isn't the only way to write. Here are a few other journal styles:

- **Bullet journal:** Fill blank pages with quick lists, whether you're control-freak organized or creatively chaotic.
- **Astrology journal:** Navigate daily events, weekly plans, and monthly goals with an eye on the stars. Note moods, moon phases, habits, and horoscope insights.
- **Garden journal:** Prep for plantings; sketch your dream design; track progress of fruits, veggies, and herbs; and press flowers into the pages.
- **Student journal:** Plan schedules, track study habits and grades, and note assignments, quizzes, and tests.
- **Travel journal:** Map out your trip from research to packing lists and itineraries. Post-trip, transform your plan into a scrapbook with photos and mementos.

4 Soothing Homemade Lotion Bars

By adding a few ingredients to a simple base, you can make a variety of moisturizing bars to soothe your skin. To make the base, melt 5 tablespoons of cocoa butter and 2 teaspoons of safflower oil in a double boiler. Pour the liquid into a mold or ice cube tray. Next, add one of these options, then refrigerate until solid:

1. **Rose lotion bar:** rose essential oil and rose petals.

2. **Lavender lotion bar:** lavender essential oil and dried lavender buds.

3. **Lemon lotion bar:** lemon essential oil and dried lemon zest.

4. **Vanilla lotion bar:** vanilla essential oil.

4 Delicious Lip & Skin Scrubs

These mixtures will keep your lips, hands, and body smooth—gently rub them into skin, then rinse and moisturize.

1. **Vanilla latte scrub:** Mix together ¼ cup brown sugar, 2 tablespoons coffee grounds, 3 tablespoons olive oil, and ¼ teaspoon vanilla extract.

2. **Pink rose scrub:** Mix together ⅓ cup Himalayan pink salt, 2 tablespoons coconut oil, and a few drops rose essential oil.

3. **Sweet mint scrub:** Mix together ⅓ cup cane sugar, 1½ tablespoons olive oil, 2 teaspoons honey, and ¼ teaspoon peppermint extract.

4. **Coconut vanilla scrub:** Mix together ½ cup brown sugar, 3 tablespoons coconut oil, and ¼ teaspoon vanilla extract.

4 Beautiful Handmade Soaps

These soaps are good for your skin and pretty enough to give as gifts. All of them start with an unscented soap base (widely available online), which gets melted down and molded, then allowed to set at room temperature.

1. **Rose soap:** Stir together ¾ cup sugar (gently exfoliates skin), ¼ cup dried rose petals, ¼ cup coconut oil (moisturizes skin), and 1½ tablespoons rose water (soothes irritation). Add ¾ cup soap base (reduces oil buildup). Pour into a soap mold or ice cube tray until set.

2. **Green tea soap:** Mash together ¾ cup sugar, 2 tablespoons green tea leaves (reduces inflammation), ¼ cup coconut oil, 1 tablespoon honey (hydrates and soothes skin), and 15 drops lemon essential oil (may lighten dark spots). Add ¾ cup soap base. Pour into a soap mold or ice cube tray until set.

3. **Lavender soap:** Mash together ¾ cup sugar, ¼ cup lavender buds, ¼ cup coconut oil, and 15 drops lavender essential oil (soothes skin, reduces scarring). Add ¾ cup soap base and optional ¼ teaspoon mica dye (a colored powder made from naturally occurring minerals) for purple color. Pour into a soap mold or ice cube tray until set.

4. **Charcoal soap:** Mash together ¾ cup sugar, ¼ cup coconut oil, and ⅛ teaspoon activated charcoal (absorbs dirt and oil, exfoliates, targets acne). Stir in ¾ cup soap base. Pour into a soap mold or ice cube tray until set.

Soothe Sensitive Skin with a Homemade Oatmeal Body Scrub

Besides being a breakfast food, oatmeal also moisturizes, exfoliates, and reduces skin inflammation. Reap those benefits with this easy DIY recipe: Blend ½ cup uncooked rolled oats in a blender. Then mix with ½ cup brown sugar, 1 cup coconut oil, and 2 tablespoons olive oil. Place in an airtight container and use for 2–4 months.

CHAPTER 6

Gardening & Outdoors

EARN YOUR GREEN THUMB

This chapter will help get you ready to manage your little slice of the great outdoors, whether it's a potted balcony **garden** or a sprawling lawn. It has basics for new homeowners; tips, tricks, and hacks for maintaining your yard; and creative inspiration for decorating your home's exterior. Because **nature** is ever-changing, keeping up with your flower beds and your front porch is a never-ending process. But over time, you can develop the skills and confidence you need to make your garden bloom.

Gardening for Beginners

Thinking of getting your thumb a little green? Here are a few things to know:

- **Be realistic.** Learning what grows well in your region and on your property will help you avoid disappointment.

- **Learn what your soil is like.** It's not all just indistinguishable dirt; it can vary widely, depending on many factors, and there are things you can do to change it. (Ask your local garden center for help!)

- **You don't need to plant seeds.** Know that while growing plants from seeds can be fun, for some varieties, it's easier to start with transplants.

- **Make a plan.** Gardening is not a hobby for the impulsive: You'll need to map out your garden physically as well as temporally (like, over months and years).

- **Be prepared to keep it up.** It depends on what you plant, but some plants are sort of like pets in that you'll need someone who can feed and care for them if you go away.

Know the Difference Between Perennials and Annuals

Like stalactites and stalagmites, it can be embarrassingly difficult to remember which is which. So here it is:

- **Perennials** regrow every year (for years, but not for eternity).
- **Annuals** live for just one growing season, then they die.

Annuals tend to have a longer growing season than perennials. You can totally combine both in your garden. Many colorful summer favorites, like zinnias and marigolds, are annuals. Some flowers that reliably bloom every spring, like tulips and daffodils, are perennials.

Know Your Zone

If you're new to gardening, you can save yourself a lot of failed attempts by knowing the climate and conditions of your region. In the United States, the shortcut to these can be found on the USDA Plant Hardiness Zone Map, which divides the nation into numbered areas. Once you know your zone, you'll be able to check which plants will thrive in your location—and which will struggle. Visit USDA.gov to see where you are.

Own These Basic Gardening Tools

Before you fill your cart with specialized items you may not even use, here are some basics to stock up on:

- A rake for cleaning up fallen leaves.
- A lawn mower for maintaining your grass. (If you only have a tiny patch of green, a weed whacker might be all you need.)
- A snow shovel (if it ever snows in your area).
- A broom for sweeping leaves and debris from your front steps, walkway, or porch.
- A heavy tarp or two for covering items outside in the rain, even temporarily.
- A long extension cord for any electronics you take outside.
- Paper yard bags for leaves, twigs, and other yard waste.
- Work gloves for protecting your hands from blisters, bugs, poison ivy, and so much more.
- Clippers or pruners for snipping little branches that go rogue.

4 *Backyard Pool Noodle Hacks*

These bendy floaty tubes are very versatile, which shapes up to look like backyard fun for all ages.

1. Make a sprinkler. Cut off one end of a noodle, stuff the end in the hole to block it, then tape it closed. Insert a hose into the other end and tape in place. Poke holes along one side, then turn on the water.

2. Make a floating table. Cut four sections of noodle, slit the pieces lengthwise so they fit over the cutting board edges, and then slip noodles over the edges of the cutting board. Put it in the pool, sit some drinks on it, and gather 'round!

3. Corral pool toys in the water. Slice a noodle lengthwise and slip it around the rim of a plastic laundry basket.

4. Blow bubbles! Slice a 1-inch cross section of pool noodle and dip in soapy water.

Assess Outdoor Space When You're House Hunting

When you look at houses, it's natural to concentrate on the living space. But don't ignore the exterior. Here are some ways to determine the condition of the house's outside space:

- Check how close tree limbs are to the house, including those from neighbors' trees. Also look for dead trees (or listen: Woodpeckers are a hint).

- If possible, visit the property after it rains. You'll see if water pools near the house (not good for the foundation) and notice signs of flooding.

- Note the size and slope of the lawn and whether there are hedges or bushes.

- Check out the condition of sidewalks, driveways, and other paved areas where you'll be responsible for snow removal.

- If there's a garden or plantings, ask yourself if you'll want to keep it up, change it, or rip it out. All involve varying amounts of time and money.

Delay Bolting

What in the world is bolting and why do I want to delay it, you ask? When someone says their lettuce or spinach has bolted, aka gone to seed, it means the plant has suddenly grown a flower stalk and produced seeds. At this point, the vegetables, the parts you want to eat, stop growing. Bolting is totally normal; it's just what plants do to survive. But it's a process you want to delay in your own garden in order to harvest more edible veggies. You can do this, or try to, by selecting plants carefully, timing planting right, and keeping them fed and cared for properly.

Revive a Sad Plant

Maybe you got busy and neglected your plant or went away and came back to find it wilting in despair. It might be a lost cause—but it might not! Try this process to save it.

First, remove the plant from its pot and soak dry roots in water for 15–20 minutes to rehydrate. Then remove any dead leaves. Finally, replant in new soil. Place the plant in the correct environment, and water it according to the instructions on the tag. Then be patient for a few days: It might perk right up again.

Transfer a Houseplant to the Garden

You have a plant *inside* your house. You want it to be *outside* your house. Here's how to get it there:

- **Make sure the conditions are right.** Do some research to determine whether your plant can thrive outside given the climate and weather where you live.
- **Gradually expose plants to sun and wind.** Move them to brighter spots in the house and give them some sheltered time outside before permanently moving them to the garden. This acclimates them to their new environment.
- **Be gentle.** Dig a hole in your garden, then slowly remove the plant from its pot, sliding it out rather than pulling. Loosen the roots carefully, releasing them if they've molded to the shape of their pot. Place the roots in the ground, filling in and patting down soil as needed.
- **Treat your plant right.** Water it once it's planted, then make sure you keep up with its care.

Fix Root-Bound Plants

Root-bound refers to when a plant's roots have become tangled and packed together. You've probably seen this if you've bought plants from the super-market in little plastic pots. Sometimes, when you remove the plant, you find its roots look like a pot-shaped mass or have wound themselves through the drainage holes. (The condition is also sometimes called "pot-bound.") You can often fix the issue by gently loosening roots by hand or with a knife before replanting.

Deadhead Your Flowers

It sounds morbid, but deadheading simply refers to removing the dead flower heads from a plant. Which is slightly morbid, in a way, but it helps your plants live their best life by encouraging them to continue growing. If you dead-head when you see flowers shrivel up, you should see your flowering plants flourish, growing back fuller than before.

Food to Keep Your Plants Happy

Turns out plants like the same foods people do! Here are some scraps you can reuse in the garden:

- Sprinkle crushed eggshells on soil to give plants calcium to grow. Bonus: It deters pests!
- Shake some cinnamon on soil to boost root growth and fight mold.
- Orange peels boiled with water and a little dish soap make an effective spray to fight off bugs and slugs that love leaves in your garden.
- Pomegranate peel chopped and blended with water makes a nutrient-rich food for plants when applied to the soil.
- Banana peels are also packed with nutrients. Dry them in the sun and crush them into fertilizer to help plants flourish.

Light the Way

Even if you do nothing else to spruce up your outdoor space, adding some lights can make a huge impact. Whether you like lanterns, string lights, votives in Mason jars, or other forms of illumination, introducing these to your yard can totally switch up the feel of your space.

Consider Composting

One method to make your garden grow (and reduce waste) is to compost your kitchen leftovers. (If you don't have space outdoors, it's not a problem; you can compost outdoors or indoors with the right equipment.) By collecting fruit and vegetable scraps, along with lawn clippings, leaves, and other organic materials, you can produce a natural fertilizer that will enrich your soil and make your plants happy. If you've never tried it, composting can seem complicated, but there are lots of resources out there, from local governments and businesses to nonprofits and individuals who enjoy educating people on the process. So seek out some info specific to your situation (indoors, outdoors, etc.) before you just start throwing cucumber peels in a bucket.

By the way, you'll be helping the environment while you're at it: Among other benefits, composting keeps greenhouse gas–generating waste out of landfills.

Use Storage Caddies

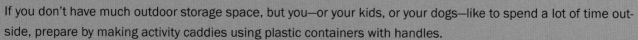

If you don't have much outdoor storage space, but you—or your kids, or your dogs—like to spend a lot of time outside, prepare by making activity caddies using plastic containers with handles.

You can fill one with sunscreen, a hat, and garden tools. Or with picnic supplies, minus the food. Or with TBR books and beach towels. Or with chalk, bubbles, and other small toys. You get the idea.

Store your caddies inside, ideally near the door, then just grab one and go the next time you're headed outside.

Clean a Nasty Garbage Can

There's no way around it. Eventually, your outdoor garbage can will start to smell. Here's how to get it clean:

- Tip the can over and empty it of every scrap of everything. Then rinse it inside and out with water, using a hose or a bucket. Then get some all-purpose cleaner or mix a dash of dish soap in water. (You can also make a solution of dish soap, water, and white vinegar for added odor fighting.)
- Scrub the can with a long-handled scrub brush or an old stiff-bristled broom.
- Rinse with water, then leave the can to dry with the lid open.

    If that doesn't do it, pour a few cups of white vinegar in the can and let it soak for several hours. Or pour in some baking soda and leave overnight, then rinse and dry again.

Make Your Own Outdoor Furniture Cleaner

Patio furniture can get quite dirty out there in the elements. Here's how to refresh it so it looks inviting again. Add $\frac{1}{2}$ cup of white vinegar, 1 cup of club soda, 1 cup of dish soap, and 15 drops of essential oil to a spray bottle and shake. Spray cleaner on furniture, then scrub with a scrub brush. Wipe suds away and polish with a clean cloth.

Salvage Rusty Garden Tools

If your shovels and clippers are rusty, don't give up on them. Spray white vinegar on metal, then wrap the tools in paper towels and place in a plastic container. Spray again until the paper towels are saturated and let sit for 2 hours. Wearing rubber gloves, remove the paper towels and scrub the metal with a toothbrush. Then rinse with water, put tools back in the container, and sprinkle with baking soda. Add a few inches of water. Scrub tools again, then rinse and dry them. Finally, coat them with mineral oil.

Personalize Your Space

It might sound obvious, but when you're planning out your exterior space, remember to build the backyard of *your* dreams and not someone else's. Not into grilling or parties? Skip the outdoor kitchen and instead chill all weekend under the trees sprawled on your outdoor daybed. Not interested in gardening? Perhaps you'd prefer ground cover you don't have to manage.

Class Up Your Front Entry

Unsure how to improve the look of that quasi-room outside your door? Make minimal changes for maximum impact. Here are some ideas:

- Instead of cluttering with decorations, pick one statement piece, like a gorgeous wreath for the door.
- Find simple seasonal switches you can make to the same place or item, like swapping throw pillow covers and putting out special doormats.
- Choose front-door necessities wisely, and your house numbers, door knocker, and lighting will show off your style without the need for extra decorations.
- Turn to nature (e.g., pumpkins, flowers, and greenery) for easy and eco-friendly seasonal outdoor decor.

Use Color to Add Character

A shortcut to an eye-catching outdoor space full of conversation starters is to brighten up your garden with colorful items. Paint pots, furniture, and decorations in your favorite color scheme to create a look unique to you.

Small Space Gardening Ideas

Working with a small outdoor space? Have no fear—the end result can be just as relaxing and enjoyable as a more expansive space. Here are some possibilities:

• Plant vertically. For example, stand a wooden pallet upright and fill it with landscaping fabric, soil, and greens. Or consider wreaths or trellises that might fit better than planters.

• Choose small plants in small containers to keep the scale in line, such as succulents in a cinderblock.

• Make use of walls and fences. They can support storage shelves that might be in a shed or garage elsewhere.

• Go big (in a small way). Having a mini-yard makes it easier and less expensive to implement a major—or unusual—change, like swapping grass for a wildflower meadow or brick patio.

Make a Small Porch or Balcony Feel Spacious

If your porch, patio, or balcony is tiny, you can make it feel roomier with a few not-so-tricky tricks:

• Use an area rug to divide the space (e.g., to denote a seating area) without taking up space.

• Choose L-shaped furniture to maximize corners and leave more room in the center of the space.

• Pick furniture with built-in storage.

• Go with folding tables and chairs over regular options.

• Split up the space with plants. Airier than furniture, they won't add bulk or look out of place outdoors.

• Attach window boxes to porch or balcony railings to provide a garden feel without overwhelming your space.

• Hang plants or decorative items from the ceiling to fill otherwise unused vertical space.

Organize Your Gardening Tools

Dirt is messy, but gardening tools don't have to be.

- Store tools metal side down in a bucket of sand mixed with mineral oil. It keeps them sharp and rust-free.
- Keep seed packets in the plastic sleeves of an old photo album or CD case. Extra credit: Alphabetize them.
- Use gumball machine–style dispensers for seeds and fertilizers. Mess-free and portion-controlled.
- Save plant tags, punch a hole in the pointy end, and feed a large paper clip through it. Hang tags from small hooks on the edge of a shelf in your garden shed to remember what you planted.
- Use a pegboard and nails to hang work gloves, tools, and other easily misplaced items.
- Store heavy bags of soil in airtight wheeled bins. They'll stay fresh and bug-free and are easily moved where you need them.

Grow Your Own Potatoes

Like farm-to-table, but your yard is the farm.

- With a utility knife, cut a rectangle out of one side of a large plastic pot. (Leave the rim and base intact.) Use the cut-out piece to trace an identical rectangle on the three other sides of the pot and cut these out as well.
- Place the pot inside another pot just large enough to hold it.
- Add 4 inches of soil, then add four seed potatoes. Add another layer of soil, then water.
- As sprouts appear, cover them with more soil, and water them. Repeat until the pot is full.

    After 3 months, pull out the inner pot and harvest your taters!

Fill a Planter Properly

Filling up an outdoor planter is super simple, and you don't need to be a pro gardener to do it. First, fill the planter with potting mix, using a trowel. Fill the pot up to a few inches from the top. Gently pull your new flowers out of their plastic pots or trays. Use your hands to loosen the roots and soil so the bottom of the plant looks raggedy. Dig a little recess for each plant in the potting mix, and nestle it inside so the flowers and leaves are fully above the soil and sticking up from the planter how you want them. Place in or out of sun as directed.

Use Aluminum Foil Outside

Aluminum foil has a surprising amount of hacks for the great outdoors:

- Use foil to frighten birds that want your vegetables. Hang pieces of foil or mix them with your mulch. You can also wrap it around the stems of plants to ward off cutworms.
- Clean your grill post-BBQ using balled-up foil as a scrub brush.
- Harness the sun's heat for your plants by lining a box with foil and filling it with pots for newly planted seeds.
- Scare off slugs by laying flat sheets of foil around the base of a plant. (Weigh it down with stones.)

Understand What Heirloom Means

Think heirloom, and you probably picture the cool-looking tomatoes at the farmers' market. But heirloom is a term that can apply to fruits, vegetables, flowers, and seeds. It basically means an open-pollinated (i.e., pollinated naturally by wind and insects) cultivar (or variety) that's been traditionally, and not commercially, grown for a long time. That said, the definition of heirloom is debated, so you might hear gardeners disagree about what qualifies.

Build Your Own (Simple, Affordable) FIREPIT

Firepits have been on quite the journey, from primitive need to backyard trend to outdoor entertaining standby. If you've ever wanted one but thought they were crazy expensive or difficult to DIY, think again. You can in fact construct your own firepit. Here's how.

WHAT YOU NEED:

- 39 retaining wall blocks
- 30 retaining wall block caps (optional)
- 2 bags of gravel
- 1 bag of sand
- Construction adhesive
- Shovel

HOW TO DO IT:

1. Measure out a circle using 10 blocks.

2. Cut around it in the grass with the shovel, then remove blocks.

3. Dig a hole 6 inches deep.

4. Level dirt with a tamper or other heavy flat object.

5. Dump the sand into the pit and spread evenly until surface is flat.

6. Place 10 blocks around the hole's inner edge and tap with a rubber mallet to set.

7. Cover blocks with construction adhesive and add a second row, staggering bricks so the cracks don't line up.

8. For the second row only, use 9 bricks instead of 10. Leave three gaps evenly spread around the circle, about 3 fingers wide, so the fire can breathe and let in proper airflow.

9. Repeat for the next two rows, minus the gaps.

10. Add an optional top layer using 30 retaining wall block caps and adhesive.

11. Fill the pit with gravel, nearly burying the first row of bricks, to help drain rainwater.

12. Spread gravel around the outer edges of your firepit to protect surrounding grass.

Make Your Own
Garden Pest Solutions

Keep the usual suspects away from your garden with these handy homemade hacks:

- Use the feet from old tights to wrap individual apples on the tree to protect them from moths and worms.
- Sprinkle coffee grounds on soil around plant roots to deter mosquitos and slugs.
- Stand chopsticks or plastic forks upright in the soil of flower beds to ward off neighborhood cats or bunnies.
- Mix 2½ cups water, ½ cup cooking oil, and ¾ tablespoons dish soap. Spray on stems and leaves to repel aphids, white flies, and spider mites.
- Mix 3 cups water and 1 tablespoon baby shampoo to manage aphids, white flies, spider mites, scale, and thrips.
- Repel munchy mammals by combining half a chopped onion, 5 garlic cloves, ½ teaspoon cayenne pepper, and 3 cups boiling water. Let sit for 1 hour, then strain. Spray liquid on fruits and vegetables.

Make Your Own Weed Killer

Skip the store-bought stuff and weed out weeds with this DIY solution. Mix 3 cups of white vinegar with ¼ cup of salt and ½ teaspoon of dish soap. Pour into a spray bottle. Spray directly on weeds.

Take Safe Storage Seriously

If you store pesticides, fuel, or other chemicals in your garage, shed, or elsewhere outside, make sure it's all secured where kids, pets, or wild critters can't access them. Also ensure that anything that needs to be in a ventilated space or certain temperature range is stored properly. Bonus tip: Keep products in original containers, or at least label containers clearly.

Defeat Mosquitoes in Your Yard

To deter annoying (and disease-spreading) mosquitoes, be on the lookout for standing water around the outside of your home. If rainwater pools in flowerpots, or on outdoor furniture or tarps, pour it out. And if possible, tip water-collecting objects upside down before a rainstorm.

Don't Eat Random Wild Plants

If you find something that sorta looks edible growing in your yard—and you didn't plant it—proceed with the utmost caution. Unless you're very experienced with wild plants or have an expert friend who can advise you, it's not worth the risk of consuming something that looks "just like" a harmless mushroom from the grocery store, but isn't.

Common Harmful Plants to Avoid

Many plants are harmful if ingested, but some are so savage they shouldn't even be touched. Learn what those native to your area look like so you can steer clear of them as you work your little bit of land.

- **Poison ivy and poison oak:** There's a reason someone coined the phrase "Leaves of three, leave them be."

- **Poison sumac:** Looks lovely, is not lovely.

- **Giant hogweed:** Looks cool, is terrifying.

- **Wild parsnip:** Looks sweet, is toxic.

- **Monkshood:** You can look, but you can't touch.

- **Stinging nettle:** Not all nettles sting, but don't touch them to find out.

- **Burrs:** Not a plant but a spiky seed or fruit produced by many types of plant, these prickly little guys aren't seriously harmful, but can be very painful and annoying if they latch on to you or a pet.

5 Low-Maintenance Yard and Garden Ideas

If your landscaping mood is "set it and forget it," consider these alternatives to the constant maintenance life:

1. Xeriscaping: Xeriscaping is a form of landscaping that requires little or no irrigation. Popular in arid and drought-prone areas, xeriscaping reduces or eliminates grass and helps conserve water, which means less mowing and watering for you!

2. Patios: Replacing your lawn with brick or stone can be pricey, but once it's done, you won't have to deal with grass.

3. Gravel, pebbles, or rocks: Covering a large or small portion of your yard with loose stones is another way to cut down (no pun intended) on lawn care.

4. Add a pond: This option wouldn't work everywhere, but how cool would that be?

5. Artificial grass: It just rolls out and stays there, perfect, all the time.

Decide If You Need Mulch

Mulch is not a specific material but a name for anything that's spread over soil as a covering. It can be natural, made from tree bark, leaves, grass, or straw. It can also be synthetic. It retains moisture, moderates soil temperatures, and stops weeds from growing, among other benefits. It can also make a landscape look more polished; you've undoubtedly seen it without really noticing it around trees and along walkways. Check out your space and decide if mulch might help your plants thrive or improve the look of your planting areas.

Transform Your Backyard in 48 Hours

When you want your yard to look better *fast*, try these relatively quick fixes that can make a huge difference:

- **Clean, clear, declutter.** Pull weeds, rake leaves, remove trash and random objects lying around, and take away furniture or decorations you don't like.
- **Consider sod.** It's the only way to get that perfect lawn instantly, and though you have to prep the ground first, you won't have to wait for grass to grow.
- **Power wash stone pavers.** It's a simple refresher for any outdoor area.
- **Create a small garden.** You can't grow a full garden overnight, but you can make a little section bloom with potted plants or a border.
- **Add a focal point for entertaining.** Something like a firepit or movie projector screen is always a hit at outdoor parties.
- **Get furniture.** Either buy new or used, or make over existing pieces with paint and weather-resistant upholstery fabric.
- **Introduce lighting.** Try string lights, lanterns, or (carefully watched) candles.

Upcycle Old Tires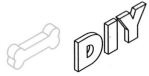

If your tires are tired, don't let them sit in a landfill when you replace them. Instead, use them in your outdoor space! Here are a few ideas:

- Perk them up with a coat of spray paint and stack them one on top of the other. Then place a round "tabletop" over them for a combo mini-outdoor table and storage.
- Or fill one tire with a soft blanket and make an outdoor bed for your small dog.
- Or fill with soil and add plants!

Regrow Your Own Herbs & Spices

If you buy these herbs at a grocery store for a recipe but don't use them all, you can replant them to grow fresh versions:

- **Cilantro:** Cut 3 inches from bottom. Place standing up in a glass with a small amount of water, and transfer to soil after roots grow 2 inches.
- **Lemongrass:** Cut 3 inches from bottom. Place standing up in a glass with a small amount of water, and transfer to soil after 2 inches of growth.
- **Garlic:** Plant cloves several inches apart in soil.

- **Rosemary:** Strip a few sprigs so only the top leaves remain. Stand upright in a tin can. Add water. Transfer to soil when roots grow.
- **Ginger:** Cut two small chunks, leaving 2–3 buds on each. Soak in water overnight. Transfer to soil (in indirect sunlight).

4 Ways to Recycle Water Jugs in Your Garden

Got some old 1-gallon water bottles that won't fit in your recycling bin? Here's how to repurpose them as garden equipment.

1. Instant watering can: Poke holes in the lid, fill the jug with water, and shower your plants.

2. Scoop: Use a utility knife to cut out the side of the jug with the handle. Trim edges with scissors. For reinforcement, glue a small wooden dowel to the short side of the rectangle nearest the handle. Scoop soil from bags to pots.

3. Irrigation system: Cut out small triangles all around the jug with a utility knife. Bury the jug next to plants in your garden, then fill with water to hydrate roots slowly and evenly.

4. Sprinkler: Poke small holes along one side of a water jug. Insert a hose into the jug and secure with tape. Place the jug sideways on your lawn and turn on the hose.

Upcycle Empty Wine Bottles

Don't just drop those empty screw-cap wine bottles in the recycling bin. Instead, transform them into nice-looking plant feeders. Wash bottles and remove labels, then use a hammer and nail to punch a hole through the screw cap. Fill with water, screw the cap on, and place upside down in your planter. To add a personal touch, decorate the bottle with paint or waterproof stickers.

Give Your Garden a Summer Glow-Up

Here's a unique and modern planter project to make your garden happy in time for summer.

Spray-paint four terra-cotta pots (one large, four small) and one medium saucer. Use a fun, bright color.

Nail a 3-foot metal rod into the lawn where you want this planter to go. Place the large pot on the ground with the rod through the pot's drainage hole. Fill with soil.

Add a smaller pot, tilted at an angle, and fill with soil. Repeat with the other three pots, adding glue to secure each to the next. Tile them at alternate angles, and make the top pot sit straight.

Spread glue around the rim of the top pot and attach the saucer to it.

Now add flowers in different hues to each pot and fill the saucer with birdseed.

Your tower will attract feathered friends—and compliments.

3 Terra-Cotta Pot Projects

You could buy the pricey planters from the garden store...or you could upgrade a basic version on your own to personalize your garden however you like. Try these ideas:

1. Spray-paint inexpensive terra-cotta pots in the color(s) of your choice, and add adhesive letters spelling out the contents of each pot.

2. Make tiered planters by placing an object (e.g., an upside-down tin can) at the bottom of a large pot and filling with soil. Stand a medium pot on the object, and plant greens around the edges. Repeat the process with a small pot to top it off.

3. Create an eccentric hanging planter with a thrift store chandelier. Remove the wiring and sockets, then spray-paint the chandelier a color you love. Paint small terra-cotta pots, one for each arm, the same color. Add little plants, then attach the pots to the arms of the chandelier. Use an S-hook to suspend it.

Pot, Meet Furniture (and Storage)

Terra-cotta pots are the unsung heroes of the garden: They're tasteful, affordable, and durable, and they can be used for all kinds of things beyond simply holding your flowers. These easy backyard upgrades use unassuming pots to make storage containers that double as furniture.

To make a side table, get a large terra-cotta pot and matching saucer. If you like, paint and decorate it however you want, or leave it as is. Then rest the saucer in the top of the pot.

Glue two drawer pulls to it with industrial-strength glue, creating handles.

Now you can store garden tools, towels, or other supplies inside your pot, or use the lid as a tabletop for drinks, snacks, sunglasses, phones, or anything you need when you're relaxing outside.

To make a seat, get a round piece of wood large enough to just cover the top of the pot. Trace and cut a piece of 2-inch-thick foam to go on top.

Lay flat a piece of fabric large enough to cover the circle, then layer a piece of quilt batting material, followed by more batting material folded into a ball, then the foam cushion, then the wood board.

Pull the fabric and batting taut and use a staple gun to secure it to the bottom of the wood. Trim any excess material.

Flip your cushion over and place it in the pot to create a seat. Remove it to store items inside the pot—or to use as a knee pad while gardening!

3 Herb Garden Gifts

What's better than cultivating your garden? Sharing its bounty with others in the form of gifts.

1. The plant itself: Repot the plant in a classy pot and give it to a friend who needs a pick-me-up.

2. Rosemary simple syrup: Boil equal parts sugar and water in a pot with 2–4 sprigs of rosemary, then let steep until cool. Pour into small glass bottles. It can be used in cocktails and nonalcoholic drinks, to flavor sorbets, and in other sweet recipes.

3. Flavored olive oils: Dry sprigs of sweet basil and rosemary with lemon peel pieces on paper towels for 24 hours. Chop basil and heat on low in a pan with olive oil for 5–10 minutes. Let steep for a few hours. Repeat with rosemary and lemon. Strain oils into glass bottles.

Indoor Gardening Ideas for Small Spaces

If you don't have a garden but want to get in on that planting action, there are tons of ways to bring the outdoors indoors:

- Fill a collection of glass jars with pebbles, potting soil, and various herb seeds. Use black chalk paint and white chalk to write cute labels on each one.
- Drill holes into the tops of wine corks. Then glue small magnets to their sides. Add soil and the littlest succulent cutting into each cork, and stick on any magnetic surface.
- Hammer holes in the bottom of a tin can with a hammer and nail. Paint the can in a color you like. Fill with potting soil and flowers. Repeat to make a little flower collection.
- Collect a few attractive drink cans and cut out the tops. Then hammer drainage holes into the bottoms. Fill with soil and small cacti.

Make Your Own Living Herb Wreath

What's better than a beautiful wreath? One that's also edible.

Stuff a wreath form with coco liner, then fill with soil. Add live herbs all around and topsoil as needed. Secure with floral wire. Keep the soil moist (a spray bottle works well). Add little paper flags on toothpicks, which can be stuck into the wreath, to label each type of herb.

Hang outside in the garden or in your kitchen to easily grab a garnish when cooking.

Snow Removal for Beginners

Ah, winter snow. So pretty...until you have to remove 18 inches of it from your drIveway before work. Here are some snow removal tips, especially for those new to winter storms:

- Spread cat litter to create traction on snow. Or use anything gritty, like sand or gravel. Whatever you use, you'll need more of it in shady spots.
- If you buy ice melt, look for the pet-friendly kind.
- If your roof, or even part of it, is flat, buy a roof rake.
- Don't necessarily get the largest shovel available. Snow is often very heavy, so using a smaller, lighter shovel to lift smaller loads is easier on your muscles (including your heart).
- Fresh snow is very visible; old, dirt-coated snow, and especially ice, are less easy to spot. So be very careful when working outside (or just walking down the street).

Decorate Your Front Doorway for Winter

Let the outside of your home in on the festivities with these easy projects:

- Hang a wreath on a shiny ribbon from your storm door using an adhesive hook.
- Spray-paint plastic pots silver. Drill holes through the bottoms. Thread a thin rope through each pot and tie to a sparkling ornament. Knot the rope so the bauble hangs just below the top—now bottom—of the pot. Hang clusters of silver "bells" by your front door.

- Fill a metal lantern with shiny ornaments. Add small string lights for extra glow. Place several along your entry to light the way.
- Stack three slatted wooden baskets—large, medium, then small—so each basket rests about halfway hidden in the larger one below. String evergreen garlands around and atop the basket tower, then add candy canes or any seasonal touches you like.

Help Your Garden Withstand Winter

It's tough to get through winter, and it's even harder if you're a plant. But you can build a garden that's strong enough to survive the deep freeze.

- **Choose hardy plants.** For example, Autumn Joy sedum, Little Giant arborvitae, ornamental cabbage, and Valentina Scotch heather are both attractive and sturdy.
- **Use mulch** to limit the damage caused by freezing and thawing.
- **Use covers if necessary.** Burlap can shield delicate trees, and small plants can be covered with a weighted down pot or box before a storm.
- **Watch your salt use.** It can harm plants, so when you're covering nearby snow and ice, use sawdust, sand, or fertilizer instead.

Index

Transform Your Space—
and Your Life!

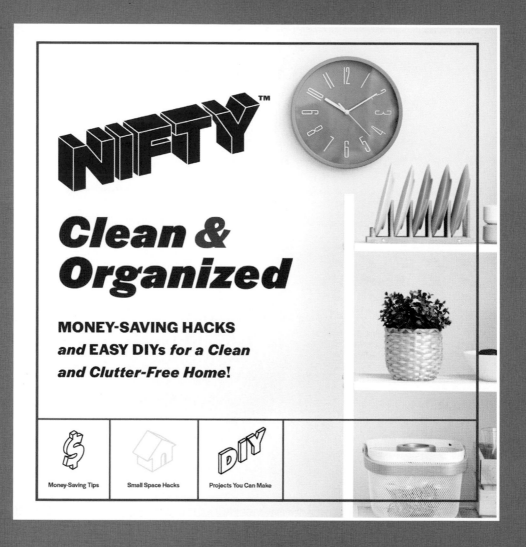

Pick Up or Download Your Copy Today!

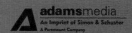